Learning How To Breathe Again

Learning How To Breathe Again

DJ Lamperez

Copyright page

This book is a work of personal experience and reflection. Any resemblance to actual persons, living or dead, or actual events is purely coincidental.

The author does not provide medical, psychological, or professional advice. The content of this book is intended for informational and inspirational purposes only. If you are struggling with mental health, please seek help from a qualified professional or licensed healthcare provider.

First Edition

Cover design by DJ Lamperez
Author DJ Lamperez

ISBN: 979-8-9952132-1-5

DISCLAIMER

This book was not written to be perfect.

You may notice moments where the grammar, punctuation, or structure feels off or different from what you might expect. That is intentional. This book was written the way I experienced life in those moments, the way the thoughts came to me, unfiltered and real. It reflects how I was thinking, feeling, and trying to make sense of everything inside my own mind.

This isn't meant to be polished or technically perfect. It's meant to be honest.

DEDICATION

This book is for anyone who wakes up already tired of fighting their own mind. For the ones who don't have dramatic stories but still struggle every day. For the ones who look fine on the outside and carry everything quietly. For the ones who never thought this would be their life. It's for those who stayed when leaving felt easier. For those who learned how to live instead of waiting to feel better. For those who are still here, even when they don't know why yet, and it's for the version of me who didn't know how to ask for help, who didn't understand what was happening, and who kept going anyway. You weren't weak. You were surviving, and now, you're living. You just have to "Learn How To Breathe Again"

DISCLAIMER 4

DEDICATION 5

CHAPTER 1 1

CHAPTER 2 15

CHAPTER 3 25

CHAPTER 4 33

CHAPTER 5 42

CHAPTER 6 62

CHAPTER 7 83

CHAPTER 8 108

CHAPTER 9 130

CHAPTER 10 153

CHAPTER 11 172

CHAPTER 12 181

CHAPTER 13 189

CHAPTER 14 198

CHAPTER 15 206

CHAPTER 16 213

RESOURCES 220

WORDS FROM THE AUTHOR 221

Chapter 1

Before the Storm – Life before anxiety and depression

I used to think I understood what depression and anxiety was. Not in a deep way, not in a way that lived in my bones, but in the way you understand things that happen to other people. I never judged it. I never thought it was weakness. I listened when people talked about it. I nodded. I felt sympathy. I believed them when they said it was heavy, when they said it was exhausting, when they said it changed the way the world looked. I just didn't know it would change my world. Back then, my mind felt like a place I could trust. It wasn't always quiet, but it was familiar.

If I was sad, there was a reason. If I was nervous, there was a cause. Feelings came and went like the weather, and I never once questioned whether the sky might stay dark for weeks, months, or years at a time. I didn't analyze my own breathing. I didn't wonder why my chest felt tight for no clear reason. I didn't wake up already tired of existing. Life felt… linear. One day led to the next. Problems had edges. Solutions felt possible. I thought resilience meant getting back up after something knocked you down, not learning how to stand while something invisible pressed against your ribs all day long. I remember hearing the words "anxiety" and "depression" and picturing them as storms that passed through other people's lives. Loud, destructive, real — but temporary.

I never imagined what it would feel like to live inside the storm instead of watching it from a distance. I never imagined the way it would blur time, distort memory, shrink the future into something that felt too heavy to look at directly. There was a version of me who woke up and didn't immediately take inventory of my own mind. A version of me who made plans without calculating emotional cost. A version of me who didn't rehearse conversations in my head or brace myself for feelings that hadn't even arrived yet. I didn't know how fragile that normalcy was, or how quietly it could slip away. At the time, I thought I was just living, not surviving, not managing, just being.

There's a strange grief in realizing that you never say goodbye to that version of yourself. You don't get a warning. You don't get a final, clear moment where you understand that this is the last day your thoughts will feel this light, this uncomplicated, or this safe. It only makes sense later, while you are looking back at how everything once was. When you're already standing in the aftermath, trying to remember what the air felt like before it became hard to breathe.

There were signs, I think. Or maybe I only call them signs now because I know how the story continues. At the time, everything felt ordinary enough to ignore. I was a little more tired than usual. I was a little less patient. There were now moments where my thoughts lingered too long on things that used to roll off me, but nothing that raised alarms. Nothing that felt like the beginning of anything permanent. I still trusted my mind. That's the part that feels the strangest to remember. I trusted it to tell me the truth. I trusted it to make sense of the world.

I didn't question every emotion or wonder if my reactions were too much or not enough. I didn't scan my own body for warning signs. I didn't live on edge, waiting for something to go wrong inside me. I moved through life without translating everything into feeling. I could be present without analyzing my presence. I could be quiet without assuming something was wrong. I could be alone without feeling like loneliness was swallowing me whole. Silence was just silence back then, not a space where my thoughts echoed too loudly. I think about how simple breathing was, or how unconscious it was. In and out, without any effort, without any fear. I never paused to check if my chest felt tight or if my heart was beating too fast or too slow. I never wondered if I was about to lose control of myself. My body and I were on the same side, or at least it felt that way.

There was also a certain innocence in the way I thought about the future. I worried of course, everyone worries. But my worries were proportional and they had limits. They didn't spiral into worst-case scenarios that felt so real they might as well have already happened. I didn't lie awake at night with my mind racing through possibilities I couldn't turn off. Back then, emotions felt like visitors, not residents. They came, they stayed a while, and then they left. None of them took up permanent space. None of them rearranged the furniture in my head. The most unsettling part is that, if you had asked me then how I was doing, I would have answered honestly: "I'm fine." Not in a performative way, and not in a defensive way. I would have meant it. I didn't know what it felt like to say "I'm okay" while quietly falling apart. I didn't know how heavy a mind could become. I didn't know that you could carry sadness without a clear cause, or fear without a visible threat. I didn't know that your own thoughts could become the loudest thing in the room, even when you were surrounded by people. I lived in a body that felt like home. I lived in a mind that felt like mine, and I didn't know how temporary that peace was.

There was a kind of freedom in not monitoring myself. I didn't measure my energy the way I do now. I didn't plan my days around how much I could emotionally handle. I could say yes without wondering how much it would cost me later. I could be tired and know sleep would fix it. I could be sad and trust that time would soften it. I think about how I used to move through the world without bracing. I didn't walk into rooms already preparing for discomfort. I didn't overthink the tone of my own voice or the expressions on other people's faces. I didn't search for hidden meanings in everything, didn't replay moments repeatedly to see if I had missed something, said something wrong, or been something wrong. Back then, my thoughts had edges.

They started, they ended, and they didn't loop endlessly. They didn't turn in on themselves. I could let a worry exist without it multiplying into ten more, with each one louder and heavier than the last. It's hard to explain to someone who hasn't lived it, how much energy it takes just to exist when your mind stops being a safe place. How exhausting it is when rest doesn't feel restful anymore, when sleep doesn't fully quiet anything, when even calm moments now carry a low, constant hum of unease. In that time before it all started, I didn't know any of this. I didn't know what it meant to feel "on" all the time, like my nervous system was stuck in a position it couldn't relax out of. I didn't know what it meant to wake up already tense, already tired, already carrying a weight I couldn't see. I remember making plans without being afraid of them. Not without doubt, not without uncertainty, but without that underlying question of whether I would even be okay enough to reach them. The future felt like something to look forward to, not like something to survive. There was a softness to my days then and even the hard ones had space to breathe.

The sad ones often had an end in sight. I didn't live in a constant state of self-awareness that bordered on self-surveillance.

I was just a person, living inside their life, not watching themselves live it from the outside. And I didn't realize how precious that was until it was gone.

I think the hardest part of remembering that time is how ordinary it was. There was nothing dramatic about it, no clear "last good day." No moment that announced itself as the end of something. It was just a series of normal mornings, normal thoughts, normal reactions. I didn't know I was living in the calm because I had nothing to compare it to. I didn't know what it meant to feel unsafe inside my own head. I didn't know what it meant to doubt my own emotions, to question whether what I was feeling made sense or if I was overreacting, under-reacting, or missing something entirely.

I trusted myself without realizing I was doing it. I used to believe that if something was wrong, I would know why. That feelings came with explanations, that fear had a source you could point to, and that sadness had a story behind it. I didn't yet understand what it meant to feel off without a clear reason, to carry heaviness that didn't attach itself to any single event. I also didn't know how much identity could be tied to mental peace. How much of "me" was wrapped up in being able to think clearly, to feel stable, to recognize myself from one day to the next. I thought those things were fixed. Permanent. I thought they were just part of who I was, the way your voice or your height is part of you. Looking back, I can see how gently life held me then. Even when it was hard, it wasn't relentless. Even when I struggled, I didn't feel trapped inside the struggle. There was space between me and my thoughts. There was distance between me and my fears. They didn't cling to me the way they would later. I didn't know how it felt to long for silence. Not external silence, but internal. The kind where your mind finally loosens its grip and lets you rest. I didn't know that one day I would crave that silence the way you crave air when you've been underwater too long. I was breathing without thinking about it. Living without studying myself. Existing without questioning the ground beneath my own emotions.

And I didn't know that all of that could change without warning and without a clear reason. Without a single moment to mark the shift. It just… slowly did.

There's a strange kind of innocence in not knowing what your mind is capable of, not knowing it can turn on you. Not knowing it can create fear out of nothing, or sadness that doesn't ask permission, or exhaustion that sleep can't touch. I used to believe my thoughts were always working with me, never against me. I didn't know they could become something I had to manage, something I had to negotiate with just to get through a day. Back then, I didn't flinch at my own feelings. I just let them exist without interrogation. I didn't wonder what they meant about me, or what they might turn into, or how long they would stay. I didn't fear my own reactions. I didn't worry that one bad day could spiral into something much bigger.

I didn't know what it was like to feel trapped inside a moment. To feel like time had slowed down in the worst way, stretching discomfort and fear until it felt endless. I didn't know what it was like to count the hours, the minutes, the seconds, just waiting to feel normal again. Normal felt like the default, not a goal. I didn't yet understand the difference between being tired and being mentally drained. Between being sad and being empty. Between being nervous and being consumed by anxiety. Those distinctions only become clear once you've crossed the line between them, once your body and mind start speaking a language you were never taught. I think about how I used to wake up and immediately step into the day, instead of bracing myself for it. How I didn't need to gather courage just to exist. How I didn't need to check in with myself to see if I was "okay enough" to function. There was a version of me who trusted that tomorrow would feel like today.

Who didn't fear sudden shifts in their own mental state. Who didn't live with the awareness that peace could be temporary, fragile, and easily disrupted. Maybe that's what makes this part of the story ache the most. Not because it was perfect, but because it was unaware. Because I didn't know what was coming. Because I couldn't appreciate the calm for what it was. I was living in it, not knowing it was something that could be lost. I didn't measure my days by how heavy they felt. I didn't keep track of my moods like they were weather patterns I needed to prepare for. I didn't wake up and ask myself what version of my mind I was going to get.

There was a consistency I took for granted, a steadiness that felt so normal it was invisible. I could sit with my own thoughts without feeling overwhelmed by them. I could be alone without my mind turning that solitude into something sharp or hollow. I could be quiet without feeling like the quiet was closing in on me. There was a difference between being by myself and feeling isolated, and back then, I still knew what that difference was. I didn't think about my heartbeat unless I was running. I didn't notice my breathing unless I was out of breath. My body didn't send me constant signals that something might be wrong. It didn't feel like it was always on alert, scanning for danger that didn't exist. There was a trust between me and myself. A simple, unspoken agreement that I would be okay. That whatever came, I would be able to handle it without unraveling.

I didn't live in fear of my own unraveling. I also didn't yet know the exhaustion that comes from pretending. From having to look normal when you don't feel normal. From having to move through conversations while a completely different one is happening inside your head. Back then, what I showed on the outside usually matched what I felt on the inside. That alignment feels rare now. Precious. I think about how I used to make decisions without second-guessing every impulse. How I could trust my reactions, my instincts, my emotional responses. How I didn't constantly wonder if my mind was exaggerating, distorting, lying. I didn't know what it was like to feel disconnected from myself. To feel like my own thoughts were strangers. To feel like I had to learn myself all over again. I was whole in a way I didn't know how to name. I didn't know how easily that wholeness could fracture.

I remember a time when the word "overwhelmed" meant too many tasks, too many obligations, too many hours in a day. It didn't mean being flooded by your own mind. It didn't mean feeling like your thoughts were louder than the world around you. It didn't mean lying awake at night, tired but unable to rest because your body refused to believe it was safe enough to sleep. Back then, stress had an off switch. You could come home, close the door, and leave it behind. You could distract yourself, laugh, lose yourself in something small and ordinary. Relief was accessible. It wasn't something you had to work for, or earn, or chase with coping mechanisms you hadn't learned yet. I didn't yet understand how heavy anticipation could become. How waiting could feel like its own kind of suffering.

How your mind could project fear forward and make you live inside things that hadn't even happened. I didn't know what it was like to constantly prepare for impact, even when there was nothing in sight. I also didn't know how much energy it would take just to appear calm. How tiring it would be to hold yourself together in public and fall apart in private. How lonely it would feel to carry something invisible that no one else could see, even when they were standing right next to you.

There was a time when I didn't analyze every shift in my mood, every change in my body, every unfamiliar sensation. I didn't google my own feelings. I didn't search for explanations for why my heart raced or why my chest felt tight or why my thoughts suddenly felt too loud. I lived inside my life instead of observing it from a distance. I was present in my own experiences instead of constantly monitoring them. I didn't know how much I would one day miss that simplicity. I think the most honest way to describe that time is that I felt anchored. Not in a dramatic way, not in a way that called attention to itself, just steady. Like my thoughts had weight, like they belonged somewhere solid. I didn't feel like I was floating through my own life or slipping in and out of it. I was there, fully.

I didn't question my right to take up space. I didn't feel like a burden for having emotions. I didn't apologize internally for being tired, or sad, or quiet. I didn't feel the need to justify my existence to myself. My mind wasn't a place I had to escape from. It wasn't something I needed to drown out with noise or distractions. It wasn't something I feared being alone with. I could sit in silence and not feel hunted by my own thoughts. I didn't know that one day, silence would become the loudest thing in the room.

I didn't know that my own brain could learn new habits—habits of worry, of fear, of heaviness—that would be so hard to unlearn. I didn't know how quickly safety could turn into hyper-awareness, how peace could turn into constant scanning, how calm could turn into something I would chase instead of something I lived inside of. There was a time when I didn't need to "cope." When I didn't have a mental toolbox. When I didn't know grounding exercises or breathing techniques or the language of survival. Because I wasn't surviving, I was just living.

The strange thing is nothing dramatic took that away. No single event that I can point to and say, this is when everything broke. It was quieter than that, slower. A shift so subtle I didn't feel it happening until I was already on the other side of it. The storm didn't announce itself.

There was a kind of safety in believing that my mind would always return to balance on its own. That no matter how bad a day felt, it would eventually level out. That emotions had a natural rhythm, rising and falling, never staying in one place too long. I didn't fear getting stuck inside of a feeling. I didn't know what it meant to spiral. To have one thought trigger another, and another, and another, until the original feeling was unrecognizable but the weight of it was unbearable. I didn't know what it meant to feel like your own head was a room with no windows, no doors, just echoes. Back then, I could sit with discomfort without panicking about it.

I could be sad without worrying that sadness would swallow me. I could be nervous without assuming it would turn into something I couldn't control. I didn't assign permanence to temporary states. I also didn't know how fragile routine could become. How even simple things—getting out of bed, answering messages, showing up—could one day feel like achievements instead of automatic parts of living. I didn't know that effort could become something you ration, something you run out of.

There was a trust in the future that I didn't have to think about. I didn't wonder if I would be okay months from now, years from now. I didn't fear that my own mind might become the biggest obstacle between me and the life I wanted. I didn't know that one day, I would look back on this version of myself with both gratitude and grief. Gratitude for the peace I once carried. Grief for how unaware I was of how precious it was. I was living in calm waters, not knowing they could turn. Not knowing how quickly the current could change. I think about how I used to make sense of myself without effort.

My reactions felt proportional. My emotions felt understandable. I didn't need to question whether I was being "too much" or "not enough." I didn't carry a constant awareness of my own fragility. There was a simplicity in the way I related to the world. If something hurt, it hurt for a reason. If something scared me, I could point to the source. My internal life had a logic to it. Cause and effect. Beginning and end. I didn't yet know what it was like to live with ambiguity inside your own mind. To feel something deeply and not be able to name it, trace it, or resolve it. To carry tension without a story to attach it to. I also didn't yet know how much of my identity would become wrapped around "being okay." How much energy would go into maintaining a version of myself that could function, that could smile, that could appear steady even when nothing inside felt stable.

Back then, I didn't think of emotional stability as something that could be lost. I thought it was just… there. Like a baseline. Like a given. I didn't know it could shift so quietly that you only realize it's gone once you're already missing it. There was a confidence in my own resilience that I didn't know how to articulate. I assumed I would always bounce back. I assumed I would always recognize myself. I didn't know how disorienting it would be to wake up one day and feel like a stranger in my own head. I didn't know that this sense of familiarity with myself had an expiration date.

There was a version of me who didn't flinch at my own thoughts. Who didn't get startled by sudden waves of emotion or how silence could stretch and press in. My inner world felt like something I could move through without fear of getting lost. I didn't brace myself before social interactions. I didn't rehearse what I was going to say in case I said the wrong thing, didn't replay conversations afterward to look for mistakes. I trusted that being myself was enough, that I didn't need to constantly monitor how I was coming across or what people might be thinking. I didn't live in a state of hyper-awareness. My senses weren't always on high alert. I wasn't constantly scanning my environment or my body for signs of danger, for changes in mood, for shifts in energy. I could simply exist without analyzing my own existence. Back then, rest legitimately felt like rest. It wasn't something I had to fight for or earn. It came naturally, quietly, the way it's supposed to.

My mind could slow down without resistance. My body could soften without fear. I didn't yet understand how exhausting it would become to carry yourself through the day while your thoughts pulled you in a hundred different directions. How heavy it would feel to constantly try to feel "normal" again, to search for a version of yourself that no longer showed up on command. I was whole in a way that didn't require effort. I was present in a way that didn't require grounding. I was calm in a way that didn't require practice. I didn't know that one day, all those things would become skills instead of states. I didn't yet know the language of mental health the way I would come to know it. Words like "trigger," "panic," "dissociation," "intrusive thoughts" were just words then. They were clinical and distant. They belonged to articles, to other people's stories, to conversations I listened to but never fully stepped into. They weren't personal. They weren't mine. I didn't yet understand how a mind could learn fear. How it could memorize it, store it, replay it without permission.

I didn't know that the body could react before the brain could explain, that a feeling could arrive before its meaning, that a wave of dread could hit without an obvious shore. Back then, my nervous system felt quiet. Not silent, but steady. It didn't misfire. It didn't sound false alarms. It didn't pull me out of the present and into imagined futures or distorted pasts. I lived in the moment without constantly being dragged out of it. I could trust my reactions. If I felt safe, it was because I was safe. If I felt calm, it was because nothing was wrong. There wasn't this gap between reality and perception, this question mark that would later hover over everything: Is this real, or is this in my mind? I didn't know how much that question would come to dominate my inner world.

There was a time when my thoughts felt like a place I could rest. A place I could return to. A place that didn't require guarding, negotiating, or calming down. I didn't have to manage myself. I didn't have to coach myself through basic existence. I simply existed. The simplicity of that, the quiet trust in my own mind, the absence of constant self-checking, is something I only learned to value once it was no longer automatic. Once it became something I had to work to find again.

I used to believe that peace was just the default setting. That your mind, if left alone, naturally settled into calm. I didn't know that for some of us, calm would become something we had to chase, something we had to practice, something we had to relearn like a language we once spoke fluently and then somehow forgot. I didn't know what it meant to feel disconnected from your own body. To feel like your thoughts were running ahead of you while your body lagged, heavy and slow, or the other way around—your body panicking while your mind tried desperately to make sense of it. I didn't know that you could feel both too much and nothing at all in the same breath. Back then, I felt grounded without trying to be. My feet felt planted in my life.

My emotions felt like they belonged to me, not like forces I had to wrestle with or ride out. I wasn't constantly trying to pull myself back into the present, reminding myself where I was, who I was, that I was safe. I didn't yet know how fragile that sense of safety could be. There was a time when my mind felt like a companion instead of a battlefield. When my thoughts didn't argue with each other, didn't spiral, and didn't collide. When fear didn't hijack logic, and sadness didn't mute everything else. I didn't know how it felt to long for your own former normal. To miss a version of yourself that still exists in memory but feels unreachable in the present. To grieve a past self while still being alive, still breathing, still moving through the world. I didn't know that one day, I would look back on this version of me and wish I could tell them to pay attention. To notice the ease. To notice the quiet. To notice the way their mind rested instead of braced. But you can't warn yourself about a storm you don't know is coming. You only learn its name once you're already standing in the rain.

I try to remember the exact feeling of waking up without fear sitting in my chest. The way morning used to feel neutral, not heavy with anticipation or dread. Just a beginning. Not a hurdle. Not something to get through. I didn't negotiate with the day. I didn't lie still, gathering strength just to stand. I didn't scan myself for symptoms before my feet hit the floor. I simply got up and entered my life. There was a time when my thoughts didn't immediately turn inward. When my mind didn't start its quiet inventory: How do I feel? Is something wrong? Am I okay? I didn't live in constant self-observation. I wasn't watching myself from the outside, measuring, evaluating, bracing. I trusted my internal weather. I didn't expect sudden storms.

I didn't carry an umbrella for emotions that hadn't yet learned how to rain without warning. And I think that's what makes the memory of that time so tender now. Not because it was perfect, but because it was unguarded. Because I didn't yet know I needed armor. Because I didn't yet know that peace could be interrupted, that stability could slip, that your own mind could become the place you needed protection from. I lived with an openness that felt natural then. An openness that would later feel risky, vulnerable, something to be careful with. At the time, it was just... being alive without flinching. There was no countdown. No sense of an ending. No awareness that this was a season that would pass and never return in quite the same way. I was standing on the shore, watching the water, not knowing how far out the tide was about to pull me. Not knowing how different it would feel to swim back. I didn't know what it meant to carry myself carefully.

To move through the world with a kind of emotional caution, like everything might be too much if I leaned into it the wrong way. Back then, I leaned without thinking. I felt without bracing. I trusted that whatever came up inside me would be manageable, understandable, temporary. I didn't have to talk myself down from my own thoughts. I didn't have to remind myself that feelings pass, that fear lies, that my body sometimes reacts to ghosts. I didn't need mantras or grounding or reassurance whispered to myself in the quiet. I didn't yet know how loud quiet could become.

There was a time when my inner world didn't require translation. I didn't need to decode myself. I didn't need to ask, what is this? Why do I feel like this? How do I make it stop? My emotions spoke plainly and my mind felt honest. And maybe that's what hurts the most when I look back. Not that life was easy, but that it was legible. That I could read myself without getting lost in the lines. That I could recognize my own reflection in my thoughts. I didn't know how much of the future would be spent trying to feel safe inside myself again. Trying to rebuild that trust. Trying to believe that calm was still possible, that peace wasn't something I had imagined, that it had once been real and could be real again. Before the storm, I didn't think about breathing. It just happened.In and out. Effortless. Unnoticed. And I didn't know how sacred that was. I didn't know all this was before the storm.

There's a strange mercy in not knowing what's ahead. In moving through life without the awareness that your own mind can become a place you have to survive. I walked through those days assuming, that whatever I felt tomorrow would make sense, that whatever weight I carried would have a name and a reason and an end. I didn't know that one day I would wake up and feel different in a way I couldn't explain. That I would start noticing my breathing. My heart. My thoughts. That I would begin to listen to my own body like it was trying to warn me about something I couldn't see. Before the storm, I trusted the sky. I trusted that if clouds came, they would pass. That if it rained, the ground would dry. That if I felt shaken, I would settle again. I didn't know what it was like to live under weather that didn't move on.

I didn't know what it was like to carry thunder inside your chest. I didn't know what it was like to look normal on the outside while everything inside was quietly shifting. I was standing at the edge of a life I didn't recognize. Breathing air that still felt light. Living in a body that still felt safe.

Trusting a mind that had not learned how to turn against itself.

The storm was not loud at first. It did not announce its arrival.

It did not ask permission. It only began as a pressure change.

A subtle heaviness in the air. A feeling that something, somewhere, was about to break. And I, unaware, kept breathing like it would always be easy.

Chapter 2

The First Crack– When Something Felt Wrong

At first, it didn't feel like a collapse. It felt like a question. A quiet, unsettled question that lived in the background of my days, easy to ignore if I stayed busy enough, loud enough, distracted enough. Something was off, but not enough to name. Not enough to stop the world. Just enough to make me pause every once in a while and wonder why everything suddenly felt… heavier. I didn't wake up one morning and know. There was no dramatic shift, no clear line between who I was and who I was becoming. It was subtler than that. A tightness in my chest that I blamed on stress. A restlessness I called overthinking. A fatigue that sleep didn't seem to touch, but I told myself I just needed a break. I kept going.

That's what I did. I kept going because that's what I had always done. Because nothing looked wrong from the outside. Because my life still moved, and so I moved with it, even when something inside me started to lag. There were moments when I would stop and realize I wasn't fully there. Like I was watching myself live instead of living. Like the world had developed a thin layer of glass between me and it. I could see everything clearly, but I couldn't quite feel it the same way. I told myself it was nothing, a phase, a tired week, or a heavy month.

I didn't want to give meaning to it, because giving it meaning felt like inviting it to stay. But the feeling stayed anyway. It stayed in the quiet moments. In the spaces between conversations. In the pauses before sleep. In the way my thoughts began to circle instead of moving forward. In the way my body started to carry tension even when there was nothing to tense against. The first crack didn't shatter anything. It just whispered. I started noticing myself more. Not in a reflective, thoughtful way, but in a wary way, like you watch something that might break if you look too closely. I became aware of my own heartbeat in moments when nothing was happening. A sudden rush of nerves before ordinary conversations. A heaviness that settled in my chest without an obvious trigger. It confused me. I had always believed that feelings came with explanations. That if I was anxious, something must be threatening me.

That if I was sad, something must have been lost. But now the emotions were arriving without their stories. They showed up uninvited, unannounced, and I didn't know where to put them. There were days when I felt disconnected from the world in a way I couldn't articulate. Not numb exactly but dulled. Like the volume on everything had been turned down a notch. Joy didn't disappear, but it didn't land the same way. Laughter felt lighter, thinner.

Moments that should have felt full felt strangely hollow. I began to question myself in small, quiet ways. Am I just tired? Am I stressed? Am I imagining this? I tried to reason my way back to normal. I told myself to push through it, to be grateful, to focus on the good, to stop overthinking. But the more I tried to ignore it, the more it insisted on being felt. There was a subtle fear in realizing that something inside me was changing and I didn't know why. Not fear in the sense of panic, not yet. More like unease. Like standing in a room where the lights flicker and you can't tell if it's a wiring issue or the beginning of a power outage. I kept telling myself it would pass. That whatever this was, it was temporary. That my mind would settle the way it always had. I didn't yet know how wrong I was.

I started carrying a low-level tension with me everywhere, like a background noise I couldn't turn off. It wasn't loud enough to disrupt everything, but it was constant enough to be noticed. A tightness in my shoulders. A shallow way of breathing I didn't realize I had adopted. A feeling of being slightly on edge, even during moments that should have felt calm. I remember sitting in familiar places and suddenly feeling unfamiliar inside myself. The room would look the same, the people would sound the same, but something in me had shifted, just enough to make everything feel a little distant. Like I was a step behind my own life, watching it instead of fully stepping into it. I tried to outthink it.

To analyze my way back to normal. I replayed days in my head, searching for what I might have done differently, what I might have missed, what could explain this quiet unraveling. I looked for a single cause, a clear reason, something I could fix, but there wasn't one. That's what made it so unsettling. There was no obvious trigger. No event I could point to and say, that's where it started. It felt like my mind had shifted its footing on its own, and I was left trying to regain balance on ground that suddenly felt unstable. I noticed how often my thoughts returned to themselves. How my attention turned inward more than outward. How I checked in with my own state the way you check the weather before leaving the house, except the forecast was always uncertain.

I didn't tell anyone, because I didn't know what to say. "Something feels wrong" felt too vague, too dramatic, too unprovable. So I kept it to myself. I smiled. I showed up. I acted like everything was fine, while quietly wondering why "fine" no longer felt like it used to. The crack was still small. Almost invisible. But once you notice it, you can't unsee it. There were moments when it felt like my own thoughts were slightly out of sync with me. Like they were running ahead, predicting things, preparing for things that hadn't happened yet. I would catch myself worrying without knowing what I was worried about, bracing without knowing what I was bracing for.

My body seemed to be responding to a danger my mind couldn't name. I started to lose the ease I once had with uncertainty. Not the big, life-changing uncertainties, but the small ones. A delayed reply. A change in tone. A quiet room. Things that used to pass unnoticed now carried weight, now sparked questions I didn't know how to silence. My mind began to fill in blanks with tension instead of neutrality. I remember thinking, why am I so aware of myself lately? Why did everything feel like it required effort? Why did being present feel like something I had to consciously try to do? It was subtle enough that I could still function. I could still laugh, still work, still show up. But underneath it all was this growing sense that something inside me had shifted its position and wasn't settling back where it belonged. I felt fragile in a way I had never felt before. Not broken. Not falling apart. Just… thinner.

Like the emotional skin that protected me from the world had worn down, and everything was touching me more directly, more sharply. I didn't yet have the language for anxiety. I didn't know what it meant for your nervous system to be on high alert. I just knew that my body felt tense even when my life wasn't. That my thoughts felt crowded even when nothing was happening. And in the quiet, in the moments when there was nothing to distract me, that question would surface again: Why don't I feel like myself? It wasn't loud. It wasn't urgent. It was just persistent.

I started to doubt my own sense of calm. Moments that should have felt neutral carried a faint unease, like the air before a storm when everything is still but charged. I would be sitting, doing nothing, and suddenly become aware of how fast my heart was beating, how shallow my breath felt, how my thoughts were quietly racing toward something I couldn't see. It felt like my mind had learned a new habit and hadn't told me about it. I tried to push it away. I told myself I was overreacting, that everyone feels off sometimes, that this was just part of being human. I didn't want to give it a name, because naming it felt like admitting it was real. And if it was real, then it might not be temporary. That thought scared me more than I wanted to admit. There were days when I felt fine, almost like my old self again, and I would cling to those moments as proof that nothing was wrong. I would tell myself, See? You're okay.

This was nothing. But the feeling always came back, quiet but insistent, like a low hum under everything I did. It showed up in the way my mind refused to fully rest. In the way I felt slightly detached from my own joy. In the way I began to anticipate discomfort even during good moments, like I was waiting for something to go wrong.

I didn't yet understand that this was the beginning of living in a body that didn't fully trust itself. That this was the start of learning how fragile a sense of safety can be, even when your life looks unchanged. The crack was still small enough to ignore. But it was there. And once something inside you starts to fracture, even quietly, you can feel it, even if you don't yet know what it means. I noticed how often I was checking in with myself, like I was taking attendance of my own emotions. Am I okay right now? Do I feel normal? Why does this moment feel heavier than it should? The questions weren't dramatic, but they were constant. A low-level monitoring that never quite turned off. It was exhausting in a way I didn't yet recognize as exhaustion. Not physical, not even obviously mental. Just a subtle drain, like something in me was always slightly tense, slightly alert, slightly preparing for something that never fully arrived.

I still moved through my days. I still smiled.

I still held conversations. But there was a thin layer of distance between what I was doing and what I was feeling. Like I was present but not fully settled inside myself. Like part of me was always watching, waiting, bracing. I remember moments of sudden sadness that didn't seem to belong to anything. Not tied to a memory, not triggered by an event. It would just rise, quietly, and sit in my chest. I would wonder what I had done wrong, what I had forgotten, what I was grieving without realizing it. And then there was the fear. Not sharp, not panicked, not yet.

Just a soft, unfamiliar edge to my thoughts. A sense that something could go wrong, even when everything looked fine. A feeling of vulnerability that I couldn't explain. I didn't tell anyone, because I didn't want to sound ungrateful, or dramatic, or broken. I didn't want to make something out of nothing. So I carried it privately, this growing awareness that my inner world was no longer as steady as it used to be. The crack didn't demand attention. It simply kept widening, quietly, while I tried to pretend the surface was still whole.

There were moments when I would catch myself longing for how I used to feel, even though I couldn't quite articulate what had changed. I just knew something had shifted, like a familiar room rearranged in the dark. Everything was still there, but nothing was where I expected it to be. I started to feel more sensitive to the world. Sounds felt sharper. Silence felt heavier. Crowded spaces made me restless in a way they never had before. Even small decisions began to carry an unexpected weight, like my mind was struggling to sort through things that once came easily. It was subtle enough that no one around me noticed. And because no one noticed, I began to question myself. Maybe this is just adulthood. Maybe this is what it means to grow up. Maybe everyone feels like this and just doesn't talk about it. So, I learned not to talk about it either. I kept showing up, kept functioning, kept meeting expectations. On the outside, nothing had changed.

On the inside, I felt like I was slowly losing the ease I once had with being myself. Like my thoughts were becoming more cautious, more guarded, more inclined to scan for danger even when there was none. I didn't yet understand that this was anxiety learning how to speak. At the time, it just felt like I was becoming more aware, more serious, more tired. It didn't feel like illness. It didn't feel like a disorder. It felt like a quiet shift in perspective, like the world had tilted a few degrees and I was still trying to adjust my balance. The crack was no longer invisible. It was just small enough that I could still pretend it wasn't there. There was a new kind of awareness settling into me, one that felt too sharp for the life I was living.

I started noticing how quickly my thoughts jumped to worst-case scenarios, how easily my mind filled empty space with worry. A pause in conversation felt loaded. A quiet moment felt suspicious. As if stillness itself had become something to be wary of. I remember trying to relax and realizing I didn't know how to anymore. I could sit, I could rest, but I couldn't fully let go. There was always a part of me that stayed tense, listening, waiting, alert. Like my body had decided it was no longer safe to fully soften. And that realization scared me in a quiet way. Because I didn't know what I was waiting for. I didn't know what threat my mind thought it was protecting me from. I just knew that the ease I once had with being present was slipping, and I didn't know how to hold onto it. I started to feel like I was living slightly ahead of myself, always anticipating the next feeling, the next shift, the next drop. Even good moments carried an undercurrent of caution, as if I couldn't trust them to last. As if I needed to brace for the moment, they would disappear. There was a sadness in that. A subtle one, but real. The sadness of realizing that something simple had become complicated. That being inside my own head no longer felt entirely safe or familiar. I still didn't call it anything. I still didn't give it a name. But I could feel the crack widening, slowly, quietly, changing the way everything felt from the inside out.

I started to measure my days by how "okay" I felt instead of what actually happened in them. A good day wasn't about laughter or progress or connection anymore. It was about the absence of that strange, heavy feeling. It was about not feeling on edge. About not feeling like something was wrong without knowing what. And the bad days weren't dramatic. They weren't breakdowns. They were just… off. Like wearing clothes that don't quite fit. Like living in a body that suddenly felt unfamiliar, like a place I had lived in my whole life but could no longer navigate in the dark. I noticed how often my thoughts turned inward, circling around my own state. Why do I feel like this? What changed? Will it go away? I tried to reassure myself with logic, but logic didn't reach whatever part of me had begun to fracture.

There was a growing sense of vulnerability, like I had lost a layer of protection I didn't even know I had. Things touched me more deeply. Worries lingered longer. Small uncertainties felt bigger than they should have. My emotional skin felt thinner, more exposed to the world. I didn't feel broken. Not yet. Just… delicate. Like something that had once been solid had begun to develop fine lines, barely visible but impossible to ignore once you saw them. I kept telling myself it was temporary. That everyone goes through phases. That this was just life teaching me something, and I would come out the other side stronger, steadier, the same. But underneath that reassurance was a quiet fear. A fear that I was changing in a way I didn't understand. A fear that I was losing a version of myself I didn't know how to get back. There were moments when I would catch myself missing a feeling I couldn't quite describe. Not happiness, not excitement, not even peace exactly. Just a sense of being settled inside myself. Of not questioning every shift in mood, every unfamiliar sensation, every quiet space in my mind. I began to realize how much energy it took to feel "normal."

How often I was unconsciously trying to return to a baseline that no longer came naturally. I would think, I just want to feel like me again, without fully understanding what that meant or when "me" had started to feel so far away. I noticed how easily my thoughts slipped into self-analysis. I wasn't just living anymore; I was observing, interpreting, trying to make sense of my own reactions. I became both the one experiencing and the one watching, and that distance, however small, made everything feel slightly unreal. There were good days. Days when the crack felt sealed, when the unease quieted and I could almost forget it had ever been there. Those days gave me hope. They made me believe I had imagined the whole thing, that I had been overthinking, that nothing was actually wrong. But the quiet always returned.

The tension. The sense of being just a little out of alignment with myself. And each time it came back, it felt a little more familiar. A little less surprising. Like my mind was slowly learning a new way to be, even as I tried to cling to the old one. The first crack wasn't a break. It was a shift, a subtle one. But it changed the way everything felt from that point on.

I started to notice how often I was holding my breath without realizing it. In conversations. In quiet rooms. In moments that didn't require tension but somehow carried it anyway. My body seemed to be bracing for something my mind couldn't define. There was a restlessness that followed me, even in stillness. I could sit, but I couldn't settle. I could lie down, but I couldn't fully rest. My thoughts would drift, not to anything specific, just around and around the same question: Why don't I feel like myself anymore? And the scariest part was that there was no clear answer. Nothing in my life had dramatically changed. Nothing had fallen apart. From the outside, everything looked the same. But inside, something had shifted its weight, and the balance I had always relied on no longer held the same way. I began to feel like I was standing on a fault line that no one else could see. The ground still looked solid. Life still moved. But underneath it, something had started to move too, quietly, slowly, altering the landscape in ways I couldn't yet understand. I didn't know then that this was the beginning of learning a new relationship with my own mind.

That this was the first moment of realizing that mental peace is not guaranteed, that it can crack without warning, that it can change without explanation. All I knew was that something felt wrong. Not loudly. Not urgently. Just enough to be impossible to ignore. I kept waiting for a moment that would explain everything. A breakdown. A panic. A clear sign that would justify the unease I was carrying. Something that would let me say, this is why. This is where it started. But that moment never came. There was no single event to hang the feeling on. Just a slow, quiet unraveling that didn't make enough noise to be obvious. It made me question my own reality. If nothing had happened, then why did I feel like something had? If my life looked the same, then why did it feel different from the inside? I started to wonder if I was just being dramatic, if I was imagining depth where there was only normal human fluctuation. But it didn't feel imagined. It felt embodied. Like my nervous system had learned a new posture and didn't know how to relax out of it. Like my thoughts had found a new groove and kept falling back into it, no matter how much I tried to redirect them.

I would have moments of clarity where everything felt okay again, and in those moments, I almost felt embarrassed forever thinking something was wrong. But the clarity never lasted. It faded, quietly, leaving behind that familiar tension, that low-level sense of unease that had begun to feel like part of the background of my life. I was still functioning. Still laughing. Still moving forward. But there was a thin crack running through my sense of stability, and I could feel it, even if I couldn't yet see how deep it went. The first crack wasn't a scream. It was a whisper that kept repeating itself until I could no longer pretend I didn't hear it.

I think what unsettled me most was how quiet it all was. How nothing around me had changed, yet something inside me had. There was no obvious loss, no clear trauma, no single moment that could explain the shift. Just a growing sense that the ground beneath my thoughts wasn't as solid as it used to be. I started to realize that feeling "off" wasn't the same as feeling sad or scared. It was more like being out of alignment with myself, like the way you feel when a joint is slightly out of place—not enough to stop you from moving, but enough to make every movement feel wrong in a way you can't ignore. I kept hoping it would correct itself. That my mind would settle back into its old rhythm. That one day I would wake up, and the quiet tension would be gone, the heaviness lifted, the sense of unease dissolved like a bad dream. I kept waiting for normal to return without realizing that normal was already changing.

The crack didn't break me. Not yet. But it changed the way I trusted myself. It changed the way I listened to my own thoughts. It changed the way I understood peace.

And even though I couldn't name it, couldn't explain it, couldn't see where it would lead, I could feel that something inside me had shifted in a way that wouldn't simply shift back. The first crack was small, but it was just the beginning.

Chapter 3

The Invisible Weight – Daily life with a heavy mind

At some point, the unease stopped feeling like a question and started feeling like a presence. Not something loud or dramatic. Just something that was always there, quietly sitting in the background of everything I did. Like a weight I carried without ever setting down, so constant that I almost forgot what it felt like to be without it. I still went through my days. I still showed up. I still did what was expected of me. From the outside, nothing looked different. But inside, everything felt heavier. Not in a way that crushed me all at once, but in a way that slowly wore me down. Like walking with a backpack, you never take off, even when you sleep. Simple things started to require more effort. Getting out of bed wasn't hard, exactly, but it wasn't effortless either.

Conversations weren't painful, but they were draining. Being around people didn't hurt, but it cost something. And I couldn't figure out why. I felt tired in a way that rest didn't fix. Not physically exhausted, not the kind of tired that comes from doing too much. It was deeper than that. A mental heaviness. A constant low-level pressure behind my thoughts, like my mind was always carrying more than it could comfortably hold. I would catch myself staring at nothing, not lost in thought, just… weighed down by it. Like my brain was full but empty at the same time. Like everything and nothing was happening in there, all at once.

The strangest part was how invisible it was. No one could see it. No one could measure it. No one could point to it and say, There. That's the problem, But I felt it in the way my shoulders stayed tense. In the way my jaw clenched without reason. In the way my breath never quite reached all the way down. It was there when I woke up. It followed me through the day. It lay down with me at night. A quiet, constant weight. I didn't know how to explain the heaviness because it didn't come with a story. There was no single thought I could point to and say, *this is what's weighing me down.* It was more like the air itself had thickened, like every movement, every decision, every interaction had to push through something dense and unseen. I could still laugh, but it felt like it took effort to reach the surface.

I could still care, but my emotions felt muted, as if they were wrapped in layers of cotton. Joy didn't disappear, but it dulled. Sadness didn't always announce itself, but it lingered in the background, coloring everything with a quiet gray. I started to feel slow inside my own head. Not in the sense of being unable to think, but in the sense of being weighed down by thinking. Every thought seemed to carry more gravity than it used to. Small worries felt heavier. Simple choices felt loaded. Even silence felt like something I had to endure instead of simply exist within. There were moments when I would catch myself thinking, *why does everything feel like so much?* Not "so much" in a dramatic way. Just… more than it should. More effort, more energy, and more emotional cost. I began to understand that you can be functional and still be struggling. That you can move through life and still feel like you're moving under water. That you can smile and still feel like you're carrying something heavy in your chest that no one else can see. The invisible weight didn't stop me from living.

It just made everything feel heavier than it used to be.

I learned how to hide it without meaning to. How to move in ways that looked normal, how to respond in ways that felt appropriate, how to laugh at the right moments and stay quiet at the right ones. On the outside, I blended in. On the inside, I was constantly managing the pressure, adjusting my posture around something that felt like it was always sitting on my chest. I became aware of how much energy it took just to be present. To listen fully. To respond thoughtfully. To stay engaged when my mind felt tired before the day had even really begun. It wasn't that I didn't care. It was that caring felt heavier than it used to. There were days when I would come home and feel completely drained, not from what I had done, but from the act of holding myself together while doing it.

From carrying the weight quietly, from not letting it show, from pretending that everything felt as manageable as it once had. I started to crave stillness, but even stillness wasn't restful. When things got quiet, my thoughts grew louder. The weight didn't lift; it simply became more noticeable. Like when the noise in a room stops and you suddenly hear the hum you hadn't noticed before. I didn't yet know how to sit with my own mind without feeling the strain of it. I didn't know how to put the weight down, even for a moment. I just knew it was there, pressing, constant, shaping the way I moved through my days. The world hadn't changed. I had. The weight began to show itself in small, quiet ways. In how long it took me to start things. In how easily I felt overwhelmed by tasks that once felt simple. In the way my focus drifted, not because I didn't care, but because my mind felt crowded, like it was carrying too many open tabs at once. I would sit down to do something and feel an immediate resistance, a tiredness that wasn't physical but felt just as real.

My thoughts would slow, then race, then slow again, caught in a strange in-between state where nothing flowed the way it used to. I wasn't stuck exactly. Just... heavy. Like every mental movement had to push against an invisible current. There were moments when I would catch myself moving through the day on autopilot. Doing what needed to be done without fully feeling present in it. Smiling when it was expected. Nodding when it made sense. But inside, I felt distant from my own actions, like I was watching myself from a few steps away. The world kept asking things of me, and I kept responding, but it all felt slightly muted, slightly dulled by the constant pressure in my mind. Even good moments carried the weight. Even rest carried it. There was no place where it fully lifted. And because it was invisible, because there was no clear reason for it, I started to wonder if it was just me. If I was weak. If I was failing at something everyone else seemed to manage with ease. I didn't yet have the language for mental load, for emotional exhaustion, for the way a mind can become tired even when a life looks unchanged. I just knew that I was carrying something heavy, and I didn't know how to set it down.

I started to lose the sharpness I once had. Not in intelligence, but in clarity. Thoughts felt foggier, slower to form, harder to hold onto. I would forget what I was about to say, what I had just been thinking, what I had walked into a room to do. It wasn't dramatic, but it was unsettling, like my mind was moving through molasses. I noticed how easily I became overstimulated. Noise felt louder. Crowds felt heavier. Even too much conversation could leave me feeling drained in a way that surprised me.

My nervous system seemed to be working overtime, reacting to things that once felt neutral. There was a constant background tension in my body, a readiness I couldn't explain. My shoulders stayed tight. My jaw ached from clenching. My breath rarely felt deep or full. It was like my body had learned to live in a state of partial defense, always a little bit on guard. And yet, I kept going. I went to work. I showed up to obligations. I answered messages. I laughed at jokes. From the outside, I was functioning. From the inside, I was carrying a mind that felt heavier with each passing week, a mind that no longer felt like a place of rest but like a place of constant effort. I didn't feel broken. I felt burdened. And I didn't know why.

There were moments when I would pause in the middle of the day and realize how tired I felt, even if I hadn't done anything particularly tiring. Not the kind of tired that comes from moving too much, but the kind that comes from *holding* too much. From carrying thoughts, emotions, worries, and unnamed feelings all at once, without ever setting them down. I started to feel like my mind was always busy, even when it was quiet. Like there was a low, constant hum of activity beneath the surface, a subtle restlessness that never fully settled. I could sit still, but inside, something was always shifting, always turning, always searching for a sense of ease it couldn't quite find.

Sometimes I would try to remember what it felt like to think without effort. To let thoughts come and go without sticking, without looping, without pulling me inward. It felt distant, like a memory from another version of myself. A version that didn't have to work so hard just to feel okay. The weight made everything feel more serious than it needed to be. Decisions felt heavier. Mistakes felt larger. The future felt closer, more pressing, more loaded with meaning than it ever had before. I wasn't just living moments anymore; I was carrying them, storing them, turning them over in my head long after they had passed. And through all of it, I kept telling myself I was fine. Because I was still functioning. Because nothing had fallen apart. Because I didn't have a reason to feel the way I did. But the weight didn't need a reason. It was simply there.

I began to realize how much of my energy was going into simply appearing okay. Not in a dramatic, performative way, but in the quiet calculations I made all day long. How much I could talk. How much I could listen. How much of myself I could give before I needed to retreat inward just to breathe. There was a constant sense of rationing. Rationing attention. Rationing emotion. Rationing patience. As if I had a limited supply and no way of knowing when it would run out, only that it felt smaller than it used to be. I started to feel guilty for being tired when my life didn't look hard enough to justify it. Guilty for needing space. Guilty for feeling overwhelmed by things that once felt manageable. I compared myself to who I used to be and wondered what had happened to that version of me, the one who moved through days with more ease, more lightness, more capacity. The weight wasn't just in my thoughts anymore.

It was in my body. In the way my limbs felt heavy even after rest. In the way my chest felt tight even when I was safe. In the way my stomach knotted over things that shouldn't have mattered so much. I didn't feel in crisis. I didn't feel like I was falling apart. I just felt… worn. Worn down by an invisible pressure that never fully let up. And because it was invisible, because it didn't announce itself with tears or panic or obvious despair, it was easy to minimize. Easy to tell myself I was being dramatic. Easy to believe I just needed to try harder, be stronger, push through. So I did. I carried the weight quietly. I learned how to live with it. Not knowing yet that living with it was not the same as being okay. There were moments when I would feel a sudden wave of sadness without a clear source. Not the kind that makes you cry, not the kind that demands attention, just a quiet sinking feeling, like the floor beneath my emotions had dropped an inch. Enough to notice. Not enough to explain. I would ask myself what was wrong and come up with nothing. My life, on paper, looked fine. There were no obvious disasters, no clear losses, no reasons that matched the heaviness I felt inside. And that made it harder. Because when you can't point to a cause, you start to question the feeling itself. You start to wonder if it's real, if you're exaggerating, if you're simply failing to be grateful enough.

I tried to talk myself out of it. *Other people have it worse. You should be happy. You're just tired.* But the weight didn't respond to logic. It didn't lighten because I reasoned with it. It didn't disappear because I told myself it shouldn't be there. It stayed, patient and quiet, shaping the way I moved through the world. I noticed how often I felt like I was carrying something unsaid. Something unresolved. A tension that didn't belong to any single thought but lived in the space between them. Like my mind was holding its breath, waiting for a release that never quite came. And slowly, without any clear moment of transition, the heaviness began to feel normal. Not comfortable. Not easy. Just familiar. It became the background to my days, the lens through which everything was filtered. The way things simply were now. And that, more than anything, scared me. Because I couldn't remember when it started. And I couldn't imagine, yet, what it would feel like to be without it.

I started to move through my days with a kind of quiet caution. Not because anything specific was wrong, but because everything felt a little more fragile than it used to. Like my emotional balance was something I had to protect, something that could tip too easily if I wasn't careful. I found myself avoiding certain thoughts without even realizing it. Letting my mind skim the surface instead of diving too deep, afraid of what might come up if I lingered too long in one feeling. There was a sense that if I opened certain doors inside myself, I might not know how to close them again. Even rest felt complicated. When I tried to slow down, the weight became more noticeable. Distractions helped, but only temporarily.

The moment things grew quiet, the heaviness would settle back in, like it had been waiting for the noise to stop so it could make itself known again. I began to understand how loneliness could exist even when you weren't alone. How you could be surrounded by people and still feel like you were carrying something entirely by yourself. Because the weight was internal, and invisible, and impossible to hand to anyone else, even if they cared. I didn't yet know how to ask for help. I didn't yet know what I would even be asking for. All I knew was that my mind no longer felt like a place of ease. It felt like a place of effort. A place where every thought, every emotion, every moment of awareness carried just a little more gravity than it used to. And I kept walking under that gravity, day after day, learning how to function with it, not realizing yet that it was slowly teaching me a new definition of what "normal" felt like.

I think the hardest part was how quietly it all settled in. There was no moment where I could say, *this is when it became too much.* No clear line between "before" and "after." Just a gradual acceptance of heaviness as part of my internal landscape. I learned how to live under it without realizing that's what I was doing. How to make room for it in my thoughts. How to carry it in my body. How to adjust my expectations of myself around it. I didn't call it anything yet. I didn't label it. I just adapted. I adapted to feeling tired even when I hadn't done much. To feeling full of thoughts even when nothing was happening. To feeling emotionally weighed down without a story to explain why. It became the quiet companion to everything.

To work. To rest. To conversations. To silence. And because it was always there, because it didn't leave, because it didn't explode or collapse or demand immediate attention, I started to believe this was simply who I was now. That this heaviness was part of my personality, my temperament, my way of moving through the world. I didn't yet know it had a name.

I didn't yet know it had patterns. I didn't yet know it could grow louder. I only knew that my mind no longer felt light. And that I was learning, slowly, quietly, how to live with the weight of it.

Chapter 4

Panic Has a Sound – Learning the language of anxiety

The first time it happened, I didn't know what it was. I just knew that something inside me had suddenly gone very, very loud. My heart started racing for no clear reason, like it had received an emergency signal my mind hadn't. My chest tightened, not in a sharp pain, but in a pressure that made every breath feel shallow, unfinished. The room felt too small. The air felt too thin. My thoughts began to scatter, jumping from one fear to another without landing on anything solid. I remember thinking, something *is wrong with my body.* Not emotionally, but physically, like I was about to faint, or lose control, or disappear in some way I couldn't describe. I tried to stay still, to act normal, to wait for it to pass. But the more I paid attention to it, the louder it became, the faster my heart went, the tighter my chest felt. The more unreal everything around me seemed.

It wasn't fear *of* something. It was fear itself, suddenly awake. I didn't yet know the word "panic." I didn't know that the nervous system could misfire like that, could flood the body with alarm without an actual threat. I didn't know that anxiety had a physical voice, that it could speak through heartbeat and breath and dizziness and the overwhelming sense that something terrible was about to happen. All I knew was that I didn't feel safe inside my own body anymore. The sound of panic wasn't a scream. It was a rushing, a pounding, A roaring in my ears that said: Pay attention. Something is wrong. Even when nothing was. It came out of nowhere., and that's what made it terrifying.

One second, I was just existing inside a normal moment, and the next it felt like my body had slammed a hidden alarm. No warning. No gradual rise. Just a sudden, violent shift from calm to crisis, like a switch had been flipped somewhere deep inside my nervous system. My heart didn't just beat faster. It *pounded.* Hard. Erratic. Like it was trying to escape my chest. Each thud felt too loud, too close, too real, echoing in my ears until it drowned out everything else. My breath shortened, then fractured, like I couldn't draw air deep enough no matter how hard I tried. It felt as if the oxygen in the room had thinned, like the space around me had quietly become uninhabitable, and then came the fear. Not logical fear. Not "I am in danger because of something." It was raw, animal fear. The kind that doesn't explain itself. The kind that just says: *Something is wrong. Something is very, very wrong. You are not safe.*

My thoughts scattered instantly. *Am I about to faint? Am I dying? Is this a heart attack? Am I losing control? Is this what it feels like to lose your mind?* The body sensations were so intense that they felt like proof. Proof that this wasn't "just in my head." Proof that something physical, something catastrophic, was happening. My chest felt tight, almost burning. My hands tingled. My vision felt slightly unreal, like the world had tilted or dimmed around the edges. The room was the same, but it didn't feel the same. It felt far away. Fragile. Like I was separated from it by glass. Time warped, seconds stretched into something unrecognizable. I became hyper-aware of everything and nothing all at once. Every sound was too loud. Every movement felt delayed. My own body felt both too present and strangely distant, like I was inside it but also watching it panic from somewhere just behind my eyes. I remember trying to stay still. Trying not to draw attention. Trying to look normal while my insides were in full emergency mode.

There was this instinct to hide it, even from myself, as if acknowledging what was happening might make it real in a way I couldn't undo. It was real and it was happening. And I had no language for it. I didn't know that this was panic. I didn't know that this was anxiety erupting through my nervous system. I didn't know that a body could react this violently to a threat that didn't exist. All I knew was that I felt like I was about to lose control of myself in a way I had never experienced before. Like my body had turned against me. Like it had decided, without consulting my mind, that I was in danger and needed to prepare for something terrible. The worst part wasn't the physical sensations, as overwhelming as they were.

It was the uncertainty.

Not knowing what was happening. Not knowing how long it would last. Not knowing if this was the beginning of something permanent. I waited for it to stop the way you wait for a wave to pass when you're caught underwater. Holding on. Counting breaths that didn't feel like they were really reaching your lungs. Telling yourself, just *get through this second. Then the next. Then the next.* And when it finally began to fade, when my heart slowly slowed, when the pressure in my chest loosened just enough to breathe again, I didn't feel relief so much as shock. Because nothing had caused it. There was no danger, no emergency, no reason. Yet my body had reacted as if my life depended on it.

That was the moment something inside me truly broke open. I realized, with a clarity that scared me, that my mind and body were capable of creating terror all on their own. That safety was no longer something I could assume. That peace was no longer guaranteed. Panic had introduced itself, and it had a sound. It sounded like a racing heart. Like shallow, desperate breaths. Like blood rushing in my ears. Like thoughts colliding in a tight, frantic loop. It sounded like my own body screaming *danger* when there was none. Once you hear that sound for the first time, you never forget it.

After the first one, nothing felt the same. Not because the world had changed, but because *I* had. Somewhere in my body, a new memory had been stored. A memory of terror without cause. A memory of losing control without warning. A memory that my nervous system would not forget, even when my rational mind tried to move on. I kept replaying it. The moment it started. The way my heart slammed. The way my breath disappeared. The way my thoughts fractured into a hundred different fears all shouting at once. I tried to analyze it, to dissect it, to make sense of it, as if understanding it would keep it from happening again. But anxiety doesn't respond to logic.

Panic doesn't care about understanding. It lives in the body. In the oldest part of the brain. In the place that only knows survival. Now my body knew something it had never known before that it *could* panic. That it could erupt. That it could turn ordinary moments into emergencies without asking permission. So, I began to listen for it. Every skipped heartbeat made me freeze. Every rush of adrenaline made my stomach drop.

Every shallow breath made me wonder if it was starting again. I became hyper-aware of my own body, like it had become a machine I no longer trusted. I monitored my pulse, my breathing, the tightness in my chest, the way my hands felt, and the way the room looked. I was constantly scanning for the first sign of another wave. And that constant scanning became its own kind of fear, because once you're afraid of panic, your body stays on alert for it. And when your body stays on alert, it becomes easier for panic to return, a closed loop, a system feeding itself. I didn't know that at the time. All I knew was that I no longer felt safe inside myself.

The world felt fragile now, like any moment could crack open into terror, or like the ground beneath my calm could drop out without warning. I started to carry the memory of that first episode everywhere, like a shadow that lengthened in quiet spaces. I would think, *what if it happens again?* My body would tense, the tension would make my heartbeat faster, the faster heartbeat would make me think, *this is it,* and the thought *This is it* would send adrenaline through my veins. Just like that, I was back on the edge, waiting, bracing and listening for the sound. I began to understand that panic wasn't just an event. It was an anticipation, a fear of fear itself, a constant awareness that your own nervous system could pull the fire alarm at any time, even when the building wasn't burning, and the loneliest part of it was how invisible it all was. No one could hear the sound I was hearing. No one could feel the internal earthquake.

No one could see the way my body flinched at sensations that looked harmless from the outside. I could be sitting still while my heart raced. I could be smiling while my chest tightened. I could be talking while my thoughts were screaming, *don't lose control.* Don't lose control. Don't lose control. Panic taught me a new language. Not in words, but in signals. In the way adrenaline tastes metallic in the mouth. In the way the world feels too sharp, too bright, too close. In the way your own thoughts become unfamiliar, hostile, urgent. In the way your body prepares for death even when you are safe. It taught me that anxiety is not just worry. It is a full-body experience, a hijacking., a false emergency that feels more real than reality itself, and once your body learns that language, it doesn't unlearn it easily. It waits, listening, ready to sound the alarm again.

What no one tells you about panic is how it changes the way you relate to time. After that first episode, the present moment stopped feeling solid. It felt conditional. Temporary. Like something that could be interrupted at any second by another surge of terror. I wasn't just living in the now anymore—I was living in the *what if.* What if it happens again. What if it happens here. What if I can't escape. What if I lose control in front of people. What if I don't make it through. My mind started mapping exits in every room. Not physical ones, but emotional ones. Ways out. Ways to disappear. Ways to get somewhere "safe," even though I no longer knew what safe meant. Because panic had taught me a brutal lesson: danger didn't need a location. It didn't need a trigger.

It could rise from inside me like a fault line splitting open. I began to mistrust my own calm. Moments of peace felt suspicious, like the quiet before something terrible. When my body relaxed, I would think, don't get too comfortable. When my heartbeat steadily, I would listen too closely, waiting for it to change rhythm. When my breath felt normal, I would test it, drawing it in deeper, checking if it would still cooperate. I was no longer just feeling, I was monitoring, measuring, and anticipating. That constant vigilance was exhausting in a way I didn't yet have words for. It wasn't just fear. It was the effort of *holding fear at bay*. The effort of trying to stay ahead of my own nervous system. The effort of pretending I was okay while my body was quietly preparing for catastrophe. I learned the geography of panic inside myself. The way heat would rush to my face.

The way my stomach would drop like I was on a falling elevator. The way my hands would tingle, my legs feel unsteady, my vision narrow. The way my thoughts would start to fragment into urgency and doom. It was like learning the early tremors before an earthquake. And once you learn them, you can't ignore them. Every small sensation becomes suspicious. Every flutter, every wave of dizziness, every moment of lightheadedness becomes a possible beginning. I stopped trusting sensation. I stopped trusting stillness. I stopped trusting myself. The world hadn't become dangerous. My body had decided it was and that decision echoed through everything. Through grocery store aisles that suddenly felt too long. Through conversations where I was only half listening because the other half of me was scanning my chest, my breath, my pulse.

Through quiet nights where I lay in the dark, afraid of the next surge of adrenaline, afraid of my own thoughts turning into triggers. Panic taught me that fear can exist without story, that terror doesn't need a narrative, that the body can scream *run* even when there is nowhere to run from. And the most isolating part was knowing that no one around me could hear the sound I was hearing. They heard my voice. They saw my face. They saw a person sitting, standing, functioning. They did not hear the internal siren. They did not feel the way my chest tightened like a fist. They did not feel the way my mind braced for impact that never came. They did not live inside the aftershock. I did. Every day. Learning a language I never asked to learn. A language made of heartbeat and breath and adrenaline and fear.

A language that said: *Your body no longer trusts the world. And it no longer fully trusts you.* Panic wasn't just an episode anymore. It was a presence, a possibility, a sound that could return at any moment, without warning, and turn an ordinary second into an emergency. And I carried that knowledge with me everywhere, like a fragile thing, like a secret I didn't know how to explain, like a storm cloud that followed just close enough to feel its shadow.

I started to realize that panic doesn't just live in the moments it explodes. It lives in the spaces between them. In the waiting, in the anticipation, and in the way your body never fully stands down from high alert. Even on days when nothing happened, when my heart stayed steady and my breath stayed even, there was still a part of me listening for the first note of that familiar sound. The beginning of the rush. The tightening. The shift. It was like living with a smoke alarm that had gone off once for no reason and now might do it again at any time.

You can't forget it. You can't fully relax. You're always half-expecting it to scream. I became afraid of my own sensations. Afraid of feeling too much. Afraid of feeling too little. Afraid of any change in my internal state, because change now meant possibility. Possibility of panic. Possibility of losing control. Possibility of being pulled back into that state where your body believes it is dying while your mind begs it to understand that it isn't. I would feel a rush of warmth and think, Is this the start? I would feel lightheaded and think, here it comes.

I would feel my heart speed up and think, *this is it, this is how it begins,* and sometimes, just thinking those thoughts was enough. Because anxiety is not just fear. It is fear learning your patterns. It is your mind and body rehearsing disaster so often that the rehearsal itself becomes the event. I didn't know then that I was teaching my nervous system to stay hyper-vigilant. That every time I scanned myself, every time I braced, every time I panicked about panicking, I was reinforcing the loop. I only knew that I was trapped in a strange new relationship with my own body, one built on mistrust and constant negotiation. *Please don't do this again. Please let me stay calm. Please let me breathe.* I would whisper these things internally, as if my body could hear me, as if it might listen. Sometimes it did.

Sometimes it didn't, and when it didn't, when the surge would rise again and the sound would return, it felt like betrayal. Like being abandoned by the one place you are supposed to be safe: your own skin. Panic made my world smaller, not physically, but emotionally. I started to avoid situations not because they were dangerous, but because they felt unpredictable. Because I didn't trust how my body might react inside them. I started to associate certain places, certain sensations, certain times of day with the memory of fear. My mind began building a map of "safe" and "unsafe" that had nothing to do with reality and everything to do with what my nervous system had learned to fear. And the cruelest part was that the fear didn't feel irrational when it was happening. It felt urgent. It felt necessary. It felt like survival.

Panic speaks in absolutes. It says *now*, not later. It says *danger*, not maybe. It says *act*, not think. Once you've heard that voice, once you've felt your body obey it without question, it's hard to believe again in the quiet, gentle logic of safety. It's hard to trust that calm is real, that peace is stable, that your own heart is not a ticking bomb waiting to go off. So I lived in between, between episodes, between breaths, between moments of normal and waves of terror. I was listening, waiting, learning, unwillingly, fluently, the language of anxiety. A language written in adrenaline and doubt, in tight chests and racing thoughts. In the constant, exhausting effort to convince yourself that you are not in danger when your body is screaming that you are. And slowly, without realizing it, I began to shape my life around that scream. I started to understand that panic doesn't just happen *to* you. It teaches you. It teaches you to watch yourself too closely, to doubt every calm moment, to question every breath, to live slightly ahead of the present, always preparing for the next internal emergency. It teaches you that your body can become a stranger. That the same heart that once beat quietly in your chest can suddenly feel like a threat. That the same lungs that once filled effortlessly can suddenly feel like they're failing you.

That your own thoughts can turn into alarms instead of guides, and once that lesson is learned, it's hard to forget. Even in stillness, I felt a subtle tension, like my system was never fully powering down. Sleep didn't always feel like rest. Waking didn't always feel like safety. There was a constant sense of *readiness*, like my body was standing guard against something it couldn't name. I began to mourn the version of myself who didn't think about their heartbeat. Who didn't notice every inhale. Who didn't associate certain sensations with danger. I missed the innocence of not knowing this language. Because once you learn the sound of panic, you start hearing echoes of it everywhere. In your pulse. In your breath. In the silence between thoughts. In the quiet moments when your mind has nothing else to focus on but itself. And that's when you realize that anxiety isn't just something that happens in moments of crisis. It's something that seeps into the space around those moments.

It's the shadow that lingers after the siren stops. It's the memory your body keeps, even when your mind wants to move on. Panic showed me how loud a body can become when it thinks it's in danger. Anxiety taught me how quiet that danger can be when it decides to stay. It settles into you. It rewires your sense of safety. It changes the way you inhabit your own skin. And slowly, day by day, you start to learn how to live with that sound in the background. Not because it goes away, but because you learn, painfully, patiently, how to breathe even when your body is convinced it can't. That was the beginning of understanding anxiety. Not as a thought, not as a mood, but as a language my nervous system had learned how to speak fluently.

A language I never asked to learn. A language that would take years to unlearn.

Chapter 5

The Quiet Fog – Understanding depression

At first, it just felt like I was tired all the time. Not the kind of tired where you stay up too late or work too much and your body just needs rest. This was beyond a different feeling especially for me. It was like my energy was gone before I even used it, but like I woke up already drained, already feeling like the day was going to take more out of me than I had to give.

I'd open my eyes and just lay there for a minute or two, not because I was comfortable, but because getting up felt heavy and complicated. The thing is I didn't feel physically heavy, like as if my body couldn't move, but mentally heavy. It felt as if my mind didn't want to start another day. Everything ahead of me already felt like it was just way too much, even if it was just normal stuff. And I kept thinking; this doesn't make sense. You slept. You're fine. You don't have a reason to feel like this. But the feeling didn't care about logic. On top of the exhaustion, I was angry. Not explosive, not yelling, not losing control. Just this constant irritation that sat under everything. Life felt annoying. People felt annoying. Sounds felt annoying.

Even silence felt annoying. It was like the world was too much and not enough at the same time. Small things would get under my skin in a way they never used to like someone talking too loudly. Someone asking a simple question, or a minor inconvenience. I'd feel this wave of frustration and think, why am I reacting like this? Why does everything feel like it's pushing on me? I wasn't mad at one specific thing. I was just mad at being here. Mad at having to exist. Mad at having to keep going when I didn't understand why everything suddenly felt so hard. And then there was the numbness that sat right next to the anger. It wasn't like I felt nothing at all, it was more like my emotions were distant. Like they were there, but behind glass. I could tell when something was supposed to make me happy, but the feeling didn't fully land.

I could tell when something was sad, but it didn't hit the way it used to. Everything felt muted, dulled, like the volume of my inner world had been turned down. I'd laugh and think, I know this is funny… so why don't I really feel it? I'd be around people and still feel disconnected, like I wasn't fully present, like part of me was somewhere else, stuck in my own head, trying to understand what was happening. The worst part was the confusion was nothing was actually wrong, nothing had fallen apart, my life, on paper, looked fine. So, I kept asking myself, what is wrong with you? Why are you so tired? Why are you so irritated? Why do you feel like you don't even want to deal with being alive right now when you know you're not suicidal, you know you're not trying to die, you just… don't want to be here in this feeling? It scared me that those thoughts even showed up. Because that wasn't me. At least, it had never been me before. I didn't feel broken. I didn't feel like I was in crisis. I just felt wrong in a way I couldn't explain.

Like something inside me had shifted, quietly, without permission. Like a fog had rolled in, and I was standing in it, trying to see clearly, and realizing I couldn't anymore. I remember thinking, over and over, I don't feel like myself. I don't know where I went.

After a while, I stopped trying to argue with it and started just... noticing it. Not in a calm, mindful way. More in a confused, uncomfortable way. Like you keep poking at a sore spot to see if it still hurts, even though you already know it does. I'd go through my day, and everything felt slightly off. Not enough to stop me from functioning, but enough that I couldn't ignore it either. Conversations felt harder to stay in. Tasks felt heavier to start. Even things that were supposed to be relaxing didn't really relax me. I could sit down, but my mind didn't settle. I could rest, but I didn't feel rested. It was like my body, and my brain were running on different settings. My body was moving through the motions. My brain was tired of the motions, and my emotions were just... flat.

I wasn't walking around crying. I wasn't constantly sad. That's what made it hard to take seriously at first. I kept thinking, you're fine. You're just in a mood. You're just stressed. Everyone gets like this. Stop overreacting. But it didn't go away. The irritation stayed. The numbness stayed. The exhaustion stayed. And slowly, they started to feel normal, which was the part that really messed with me. Because when something feels normal, you stop questioning it as much. You start building your life around it instead of trying to get rid of it. I remember catching myself thinking, I don't really care, about things I used to care about a lot. Not in a dramatic, cold way. Just in this dull, low-energy way. Like the effort it took to feel strongly about anything was more than I had in me. Even good things felt distant. I could recognize that something was good, but the feeling didn't fully register.

It was like watching happiness happen through a screen instead of being inside it. And then there was this quiet thought that would slip in sometimes. Not loud. Not aggressive. Just there. I don't really want to be here. Not in a "I want to die" way, I knew that.

I was very aware of that. I wasn't planning anything. I wasn't trying to hurt myself. But the thought still felt heavy. Like I was tired of existing in this state. Like I wanted a break from my own head. Like I wanted everything to just pause for a while. And I'd immediately tell myself; that's not you. That's not what you mean. You don't want to die. You just don't want to feel like this, but having to have that conversation with myself at all was unsettling. It made me realize something wasn't right. Because I used to wake up and just… live.

Now I was waking up and bracing myself for how the day was going to feel. And I didn't know how to explain that to anyone, so I kept it inside. I started comparing myself to who I used to be without even trying to. It would happen in small moments. I'd be in the middle of something and think, I used to enjoy this. Or I used to care more about this. Or, I used to have energy for this. And the comparison always ended the same way, with this quiet realization that I wasn't that person anymore. Not completely different. Just… dulled. I could still function. I could still joke. I could still go through my routines. But everything felt like it was happening with a layer between me and the world. Like I was present but not fully connected. Like my reactions were a second slower, my feelings a little weaker, my motivation a lot lower. I remember sitting in rooms full of people and feeling oddly disconnected. Not lonely exactly. Just separate. Like I was there physically but my mind was somewhere else, stuck in this heavy, foggy space where everything felt too much and not enough at the same time. The anger would flare up in weird ways. I'd get frustrated over nothing. Over small inconveniences. Over things that normally wouldn't bother me. And then I'd feel guilty for being so irritated, because again, nothing was actually wrong. No one had done anything to me. Life wasn't attacking me. My brain just felt like it was constantly on edge, like it had no patience left for anything. And the exhaustion was always there under it all. Not just tired, but drained. Like even thinking took energy. Like making decisions took energy. Like caring took energy. I'd look at my to-do list and feel overwhelmed before

I even started, not because it was long, but because the idea of doing anything at all felt heavy. I wasn't sad in the way people picture depression. I wasn't crying in bed all day. I wasn't completely shut down. I was just tired of everything in a way I couldn't explain. Tired of thinking, tired of feeling, tired of trying to feel normal again, and I kept telling myself, this will pass. You're just in a phase. You're just burned out. You're just overthinking. But deep down, I could feel that this wasn't just a mood. It felt like something had settled in.

There were days when I'd just sit there and stare at nothing, not because I was deep in thought, but because my mind felt tired of thinking. Like it had been running for too long without a break and didn't know how to shut off anymore. I wasn't asleep. I wasn't zoning out in a peaceful way. I was just… there. Existing. Letting time pass because engaging with it felt like too much work. I started noticing how everything felt like it took effort. Not huge effort, not the kind that makes you collapse, but this constant low-level strain. Getting ready. Answering messages. Making small decisions. Holding conversations. Even reacting emotionally felt like something I had to push myself to do instead of something that happened naturally, And that made me feel broken in a quiet way. Because I remembered when things didn't feel like this. I remembered when I didn't have to convince myself to care. When I didn't have to drag my mind through the day.

When my thoughts flowed instead of feeling stuck in mud. And I kept wondering when that changed. When did living start to feel like something I had to get through instead of something I was just in? The anger would come and go, but the fog stayed. That dull heaviness behind everything. I'd be in the middle of something and suddenly feel this wave of irritation for no clear reason. Not rage. Not hatred. Just this internal "I'm so tired of everything" feeling that made even normal moments feel overwhelming. I didn't want to talk. I didn't want to explain. I didn't even really want to think about it. I just wanted it to stop. But it didn't. It followed me into quiet moments. Into nights when I should've felt relaxed. Into mornings when I should've felt rested. It was there when I was alone, and somehow still there when I was around people. Like no matter where I went, my mind brought the same heavy atmosphere with it. I remember thinking, is this just who I am now? Is this my personality? Is this adulthood? Is this just how life feels once you grow up? The thought that this might be permanent scared me more than anything else.

The idea that this fog might not lift. That this flatness, this irritation, this emotional exhaustion might just be my new normal. That the version of me who felt lighter, more alive, more present might be gone for good. I didn't want to believe that. I kept telling myself it was temporary. That it was stress. That it was burnout. That I just needed rest, or a break, or a change of scenery. I kept looking for some external fix for something that felt internal and out of my control. But no matter what I did, the fog stayed, and the longer it stayed, the more I realized I wasn't just tired.

I was carrying something heavier than tired. I started to notice how much I was forcing myself through the day. Not in a dramatic way. I wasn't collapsing or missing everything. I was still doing what I had to do. But it felt like I was pushing a heavy door open over and over again, all day long, for things that used to swing open on their own. Getting up. Getting dressed. Answering people. Showing up. None of it was impossible. It just felt… harder than it should have. And that made me angry at myself. Because I'd think, why can't you just do this like you used to? Why does everything feel like a chore now? You're not sick. You're not injured. Nothing actually happened. So why does it feel like you're carrying this invisible weight everywhere you go? Some days I felt empty. Not sad, not emotional, just hollow. Like my reactions were delayed or muted.

Like things were happening around me and I was aware of them, but they weren't really landing. I'd hear good news and think, that's nice, but not *feel* it the way I expected to. I'd hear something upsetting and feel it, but in a distant way, like it was happening to someone else. It was like my emotions were tired. Like they had been working overtime for so long that they just… slowed down. And then there were the days when the emptiness would flip into irritation again. A short fuse. No patience. Feeling overwhelmed by the smallest things. Feeling like everything and everyone was in the way. And then immediately feeling bad for feeling that way, because again, nothing was actually wrong. It was this constant back and forth. Numb.

Irritated. Exhausted. Guilty for being numb, irritated, and exhausted. I didn't know what to call it, but I knew it wasn't just a bad week. It was starting to shape how I saw myself. I began to think of myself as someone who was "low energy," "moody," "not as fun as I used to be." I started adjusting my expectations of myself without even realizing it. Making excuses for why I didn't want to go out. Why I didn't want to talk. Why I just wanted to be alone and quiet. Not because I was depressed in the way people picture depression. But because being present in the world felt like too much sometimes. And the scariest part was how quietly all of this became normal.

I didn't wake up one day and say, I'm depressed. I woke up and said, I'm just tired. I'm just in a mood. I'm just not myself lately. And I kept saying that, until "lately" started to feel like "always."

There was a point where I stopped checking in with myself the way I used to. Not because I felt better, but because I was tired of asking the same questions and getting no answers. Every time I tried to figure it out, I ended up in the same place. Nothing happened. Nothing explains this. And that loop just made me feel more frustrated. So instead, I just pushed through. I stopped expecting to feel good. That's the part that's hard to explain. It wasn't that I felt hopeless, it was more like I lowered the bar for how I expected life to feel. If a day wasn't awful, I counted it as a win. If I got through something without feeling completely drained, that felt like progress. I didn't think in terms of happiness anymore. I thought in terms of tolerable.

Can I tolerate today? Can I tolerate this conversation? Can I tolerate getting through this week? That became the scale. And I didn't even realize how unhealthy that was at the time, because it happened slowly. One adjustment at a time. One lowered expectation after another. Until I wasn't really asking for much anymore. Just enough energy to get through the basics. Just enough motivation to not fall behind. Just enough emotional capacity to function. I remember moments where I'd think, is this it? Is this what life is supposed to feel like? Because if this is it, I don't know how people do this forever. And again, that thought scared me. Not because I wanted to disappear, but because I felt trapped inside a version of life that felt heavy and flat at the same time. Like I was stuck on autopilot, moving forward without actually feeling like I was going anywhere. I also started isolating without meaning to. Not cutting people off completely but pulling back just enough. Texting less. Talking less. Saying no more often.

Being around people took energy I didn't always have, and explaining myself took even more. So, I kept things surface-level. I told people I was tired. I said I had a lot going on. I joked about being burnt out. Those answers were easier than saying, I don't feel like myself and I don't know why. Because how do you explain something that doesn't have a clear cause? How do you talk about feeling empty and irritated and exhausted when nothing is technically wrong? You don't. You carry it quietly. And the longer I carried it, the heavier it felt. Not in a dramatic, crushing way. Just in this constant, dull way that made everything feel like it required effort. Like my mind was never fully at rest, even when I was doing nothing.

That's when I started to realize this wasn't just stress. This was something else. I remember realizing one day that I couldn't remember the last time I felt genuinely excited about something. Not fake excited. Not "this should be exciting" excited. Just real, natural excitement that shows up on its own without effort. That realization hit harder than I expected. The thing is that I wasn't miserable all the time, I wasn't constantly sad. I was still laughing sometimes. Still showing up. Still doing things. But the highs were gone. Everything lived in this narrow middle space where nothing felt terrible, but nothing felt good either.

And that scared me. It made me feel like life was slowly shrinking. Like my emotional range was getting smaller and smaller, and I didn't know how to stop it. I started to wonder if this was just how things were going to be from now on. Flat. Muted. Manageable, but not fulfilling. I also noticed how disconnected I felt from my own reactions. Someone would tell me something exciting, and I'd respond the right way, but inside I felt nothing. Or I'd hear bad news and know I should feel more than I did, but everything felt blunted, like my emotions were stuck behind a wall. That disconnect made me feel guilty. I'd think, what kind of person doesn't feel more about this? What's wrong with you? Instead of asking for help or talking about it, I turned it inward. I blamed myself. I told myself I wasn't trying hard enough. That I was being lazy. That I was just negative by nature. I didn't think something was happening *to* me. I thought something was wrong *with* me. There were moments when I'd catch a glimpse of my old self. A laugh that felt real.

A moment of interest. A spark of motivation. And for a second, I'd feel hopeful. Like maybe the fog was lifting, but those moments never lasted. They faded quickly, and the fog settled back in like it had never left. And every time that happened, it felt worse. Not because I expected to feel amazing, but because I had tasted what normal used to feel like and then lost it again. That back and forth messed with my head. It made me doubt myself. It made me question my progress. It made me wonder if I was imagining all of this. I started thinking maybe this was just who I was now. Not depressed enough to need help. Not okay enough to feel normal. Just stuck in this in-between space where life felt dull and heavy and exhausting all at once. And the hardest part was how invisible it all was.

No one could see the fog. No one could measure the exhaustion. No one could tell that every day felt like work. So, I kept going. Because from the outside, I looked fine. I didn't yet know that "looking fine" and "being okay" were two very different things. I started to realize how much of my life was running on autopilot. I'd go through the motions without really thinking about them. Wake up. Get ready. Go where I needed to go. Talk to who I needed to talk to. None of it felt intentional anymore. It just felt automatic, like my body knew what to do even if my mind didn't really want to be there for it. And that scared me in a quiet way, because I wasn't making choices based on what I wanted or how I felt. I was just doing what was expected. What came next. What kept things moving. I didn't feel connected to my own days.

They blurred together, not because they were busy, but because they all felt emotionally the same. I remember thinking, if someone asked me how today felt compared to yesterday, I wouldn't know how to answer. Not because nothing happened, but because none of it stuck. Moments didn't linger. Feelings didn't settle. Everything passed through me without leaving much behind. And I didn't know if that meant I was protecting myself or losing myself. There were times when I'd catch myself zoning out mid-conversation, not because I didn't care, but because my mind felt tired of engaging. Like it was conserving energy. Like it had decided some things just weren't worth the effort anymore. That realization made me feel ashamed. Because I cared about people. I cared about my life. I just didn't feel connected to it the way I used to. And the more disconnected I felt, the harder it became to explain myself, even to myself. I'd ask, what do you want? And my mind would come back empty. Not in a dramatic way, just blank.

I didn't know what I wanted because I didn't feel strongly about much of anything anymore. And not knowing what you want makes you feel lost in a way that's hard to describe. Like you're standing still while everything else keeps moving, and you don't know how to step back into your own life. I wasn't hopeless. I wasn't giving up. I was just existing. And existing like that, day after day, felt heavier than I expected it to. I started to feel like I was watching my life instead of living it. Not dissociating in some extreme way. Just this subtle distance. Like I was one step removed from everything. Like things were happening *around* me instead of *to* me. I was aware of what was going on, I just didn't feel connected to it the way I used to.

There were moments when I'd think, this should feel different. This should matter more. I should feel something here. But the feeling never came. And the more I noticed that gap, the more uncomfortable it made me. Because it made me question myself. It made me wonder if I was broken in some permanent way. If something inside me had shut down and wasn't coming back online. I remember feeling frustrated with my own reactions. Or lack of reactions. I'd think, why don't you care more? Why don't you feel more? Why does everything feel so flat? And then I'd get tired of asking. That's when the fog really started to feel heavy. When even trying to understand it felt like too much work. When analyzing my own emotions became just another thing draining what little energy I had left. I stopped expecting myself to feel inspired or motivated. I stopped expecting days to feel meaningful. I started measuring time in smaller ways.

Can I get through this hour? Can I get through today? Can I get through the next thing on my list? And most days, I could, but just barely. I also noticed how hard it was to picture the future. Not in a hopeless way, not like I thought nothing good would ever happen, but in a foggy way. Like the future existed, but it didn't feel real. It didn't feel connected to me. It felt distant, abstract, like something I couldn't emotionally reach. I'd think about plans or goals and feel… nothing. No excitement. No anticipation. Just this blank response. And that scared me, because I used to care about where I was going. I used to think ahead. Now it felt like all my energy was going into getting through the present. The fog wasn't dramatic. It wasn't loud. It was just always there.

The longer it stayed, the more I realized it was changing how I related to myself. I didn't trust my feelings anymore. I didn't trust my lack of feelings either. Everything felt uncertain, like I was constantly questioning whether what I felt was real, or if it even mattered. I wasn't falling apart. I was slowly disconnecting from my own life, and I didn't know how to explain that without sounding ungrateful, dramatic, or broken. So, I stayed quiet and carried it.

There were moments when I'd catch myself thinking, maybe this is just how life feels once you grow up. Maybe this is what everyone else is dealing with and just not talking about. Maybe I missed the memo where joy becomes optional, and everything turns into responsibility and exhaustion. That thought scared me, but it also weirdly comforted me. Because if this was just life, then there was nothing wrong with *me*. I wasn't broken. I wasn't failing. I was just… normal. But deep down, I knew that wasn't true. I knew what normal had felt like before.

I knew there used to be color in things. I knew there used to be moments that grabbed me without effort. I didn't need life to be perfect, but I missed feeling connected to it. And pretending this fog was just adulthood felt like lying to myself. Still, I didn't know what else to call it. I wasn't curled up in bed unable to function. I wasn't crying nonstop. I wasn't giving up on everything. So it felt wrong to say I was depressed. That word felt too heavy, too dramatic, too final. I didn't think I had earned it. So instead, I minimized. I told myself I was just tired. Just burnt out. Just in a funk. Just not in the best headspace lately. Those words felt safer. Less serious. Less scary. They let me keep going without really looking at what was happening underneath. But the fog didn't care what I called it. It stayed when I tried to ignore it. It stayed when I stayed busy. It stayed when I rested. It stayed when I distracted myself. Slowly, I started to realize that pushing through wasn't fixing anything. It was just teaching me how to survive in a state that didn't feel right. I was adapting to something that I shouldn't have had to adapt to. That realization made me feel sad in a deeper way than the numbness ever did. Because it meant this wasn't just a phase I could wait out. It meant something in me was asking for attention, and I had been brushing it off because I didn't know what else to do with it. I didn't feel dramatic enough to ask for help. I didn't feel sick enough to stop. I felt stuck in the middle, and that middle space was lonely. Because it didn't come with language. It didn't come with clear signs. It didn't come with permission to say, I'm not okay.

So I stayed quiet and kept trying to function, even as the fog slowly reshaped how I thought, how I felt, and how I moved through my days. I didn't know it yet, but this was me learning what depression actually looked like for me. Not loud. Not obvious. Just heavy. I think one of the hardest parts was how alone it felt inside my own head. Not because I didn't have people around me. I did. But because I didn't know how to explain what was happening without feeling like I was exaggerating or complaining or making something out of nothing. Every time I tried to put it into words in my mind, it sounded wrong., too dramatic, too vague, or too confusing. So, I didn't say anything. I'd think, what am I supposed to tell someone? That I'm tired all the time for no reason? That I feel irritated at life but don't know why? That I don't feel like myself but can't explain what that even means? None of it sounded serious enough to say out loud. And because I didn't talk about it, it stayed trapped inside me. I started feeling like I was carrying this private weight that no one else could see. Like everyone else was moving through life with some kind of instruction manual that I didn't have.

They seemed to handle things better. Feel things more clearly. Enjoy things more easily. And I kept wondering what I was missing. I'd look at people and think, how are you doing this? How are you just living without questioning everything? That comparison made me feel worse. Not jealous, just tired. Tired of feeling behind. Tired of feeling like I was struggling with something invisible that I didn't even know how to name yet. There were moments when I wanted to reach out. When I felt close to saying something. But then I'd stop myself. Because what if they didn't understand? What if they brushed it off? What if they told me to just be positive or get more sleep or stop overthinking? I didn't want advice. I didn't want solutions. I just wanted someone to understand. But since I didn't even understand it myself, asking felt impossible.

So, I kept doing what I'd been doing all along. I showed up. I smiled when I needed to. I answered questions with "I'm fine" because it was easier than trying to explain something I didn't have language for. And every time I did that, it felt like I was pushing myself a little further away from the truth. Not because I was lying on purpose, but because I didn't know how to be honest without sounding broken. The fog made everything quieter. Including my voice. And the longer I stayed quiet, the more it felt like this was something I was supposed to handle on my own. Like admitting I was struggling would somehow mean I was weak or dramatic or failing at something that everyone else seemed to manage. I didn't know yet that this silence was part of the problem. I just knew that carrying it alone made it heavier.

There were times when I wondered if I was just being lazy. That thought came up more than I want to admit. Because from the outside, that's what it could look like. I wasn't as motivated. I didn't have the same energy. I put things off more. I wanted to stay in more. I wanted quiet more than anything. And it was easier to tell myself I was just not trying hard enough than to admit something deeper might be going on. I'd think, you just need to push yourself. Get up. Do more. Stop being so negative. So, I tried. I forced myself into routines. Forced myself to stay busy. Forced myself to go out, to be productive, to act like everything was fine. And sometimes it worked, temporarily. I could distract myself enough to forget how heavy everything felt. But the second I slowed down; it all came back. The exhaustion. The irritation. The emptiness. It was like my mind was constantly asking for rest, not sleep, but relief. Relief from having to feel this way all the time. Relief from having to explain myself internally. Relief from pretending I was okay when I didn't even know what okay felt like anymore.

I started noticing how often I was hard on myself. How quickly I blamed myself for not feeling better. How easily I dismissed my own experience because it didn't look bad enough. I wasn't in crisis, so I told myself I didn't deserve help. I wasn't falling apart, so I convinced myself I should be able to handle it. But handling it didn't mean healing it. Handling it just meant surviving it. And there was this quiet resentment that built up because of that. Resentment toward myself for not being stronger. Resentment toward the world for continuing like nothing was wrong. Resentment toward life for feeling so demanding when I already felt empty. I didn't want to be this person. I didn't want to be tired all the time. I didn't want to feel disconnected. I didn't want to feel angry at nothing. I just didn't know how to get back to who I was before, and that helplessness sat heavy in my chest. I wasn't giving up, but I was worn down, and the longer I stayed in that fog, the harder it became to remember what it felt like to exist without questioning every emotion, every reaction, every thought. The fog wasn't just around me anymore.

It was inside me. I think what finally made it real for me was the moment I realized I didn't trust my own feelings anymore. I didn't know which ones mattered and which ones didn't. I didn't know if my irritation was justified or just part of whatever was happening in my head. I didn't know if my lack of motivation meant something was wrong or if I was just being lazy. I didn't know if the emptiness was something I needed to pay attention to or something I should ignore and push through. Everything felt questionable. I'd feel angry and immediately second-guess it. I'd feel tired and tell myself to get over it. I'd feel numb and wonder if I was imagining it. Living like that messes with you, because when you don't trust your own internal signals, you don't know how to respond to them. You don't know when to rest and when to push. You don't know when to speak up and when to stay quiet. You don't know if you're struggling or just failing to cope. I remember thinking, if this is depression, why doesn't it look like what people talk about?

Why am I not crying all the time? Why am I still functioning? Why am I still here, doing things, even though everything feels heavy and wrong? It made me feel like an outsider, even in conversations about mental health. Like my experience didn't quite fit anywhere. Too functional to be taken seriously. Too exhausted to feel okay. And that made me isolate even more, because I didn't feel like I belonged in either space. I didn't feel "sick enough" to ask for help, and I didn't feel "well enough" to just move on. I was stuck in between. I started to realize that depression doesn't always announce itself with obvious suffering. Sometimes it shows up as irritation, as exhaustion, as numbness, as losing interest in things you used to care about and as feeling disconnected from your own life without knowing why. Sometimes it looks like getting through the day and feeling nothing about it.

That realization didn't fix anything, but it did change how I saw myself. It made me stop blaming myself quite as much. It made me consider, maybe this isn't a personal failure. Maybe this is something happening to me, not something I'm choosing. That thought didn't bring relief, but it brought clarity. And clarity was the first thing that cut through the fog, even just a little. Not enough to make it disappear. Not enough to make things better right away. Just enough to make me stop pretending it wasn't there. Just enough to let me admit, quietly, to myself: Something is wrong, and I don't have to punish myself for that.

Once I admitted that something was actually wrong, I didn't suddenly feel better. If anything, it felt heavier at first. Because now I couldn't explain it away as just a bad mood or a rough patch. I couldn't keep pretending it was nothing. It had a shape now, even if I didn't fully understand it yet. And that scared me. Because admitting it meant I had to sit with it. I had to stop running from the feeling and actually notice how deep it went. I had to admit that I wasn't just tired or irritable or burnt out. I was struggling in a way that wasn't fixing itself. There were moments where I wished I could go back to not knowing. Back to when I could convince myself I was fine. Because knowing meant responsibility. It meant eventually having to do something about it. And I didn't feel ready for that yet. I still didn't know what help would even look like. I didn't know if this was something I could talk my way out of, or rest my way out of, or think my way out of.

I didn't know if it would pass on its own or if this was something I was going to have to learn how to live with. So, I stayed in this strange middle space. Aware, but unsure. Honest with myself, but quiet with everyone else. I let the fog exist without fighting it as hard, but I also didn't know how to move through it. I was still exhausted. Still irritated. Still numb. Still disconnected. The difference was that now I knew it wasn't a personal flaw. That knowledge didn't make the days easier. But it made them feel a little less shameful, and that mattered more than I realized at the time. For the first time, I wasn't telling myself to just try harder or be better or push through. I was allowing the possibility that what I was feeling was real, even if I didn't have answers yet. And sometimes, when you've been living in fog for a long time, simply acknowledging that it exists is the first step toward finding your way out of it. Even if you're still standing in the middle of it, unsure which direction to go. I didn't wake up one day and decide to call it depression. That word came later.

What I knew in this moment was simpler and heavier at the same time. I knew I wasn't okay. And I knew I wasn't making it up. The fog didn't disappear just because I named it. I still woke up tired. I still felt irritated at life for no clear reason. I still felt numb when I thought I should feel something. But now there was this quiet awareness underneath it all. This understanding that what I was experiencing had a reason, even if I didn't know what it was yet. And that changed how I talked to myself. Not completely. Not overnight. I was still hard on myself. I still doubted my own experience. But there was a small shift. A little more patience. A little less blame. A little less "what's wrong with you?" and a little more "something is happening to you."

I didn't have answers. I didn't have solutions. I didn't have a plan. What I had was honesty. Honesty that this fog was real. Honesty that it was affecting me. Honesty that I couldn't just ignore it anymore. And that honesty didn't fix me, but it kept me from disappearing into it completely. Because even in the fog, even in the exhaustion and irritation and numbness, there was still a part of me paying attention. Still a part of me that knew this wasn't how

I was supposed to feel forever. Still a part of me that wanted understanding, even if I didn't know how to get it yet. That part didn't feel hopeful, but it felt awake.

For the first time in a while, that felt like enough to keep going.

Chapter 6

Grief for the Old Me – Mourning who I used to be

I didn't know I was grieving anything at first, I just knew something felt off in a way I couldn't explain and didn't really want to look at too closely. It wasn't loud or dramatic, it was more like this quiet discomfort that showed up in random moments, when I wasn't distracted enough to ignore it, when I had just enough space to notice that something inside me didn't feel the same anymore. I'd catch myself thinking about how I used to move through life without this constant weight in my head, how I used to think about the future without immediately feeling overwhelmed or tired by it.

Back then, even when things weren't perfect, there was still this sense that life had direction, that I was heading somewhere, that what I was doing mattered in some way, even if I hadn't fully figured out how yet. Now my thoughts didn't go there anymore. Instead of thinking about goals or plans or dreams, my mind was busy doing something else, something smaller and heavier at the same time. It was always checking in on my body, my mood, my anxiety, wondering how I felt, wondering if today would be okay or if I'd spend it trying to manage another wave of panic or that familiar tight feeling that never really left. My brain wasn't imagining the future anymore, it was managing the present, and even that felt exhausting. I didn't sit there thinking, I miss who I used to be, at least not in those words.

It was more subtle than that. It showed up when I realized I didn't care about things the way I used to, not because I didn't want to, but because I didn't have the space for it. It showed up when I thought about the future and felt nothing instead of curiosity, or worse, felt this quiet dread because the future just meant more days of feeling like this. And that scared me, even if I didn't fully admit it yet. I think what made it harder was that nothing on the outside had changed enough to explain what was happening inside me. I was still living the same life, still showing up as the same person, still doing the things I was supposed to be doing. If someone looked at me, they wouldn't have seen loss or grief or anything missing at all. But internally, my world felt smaller. It felt like everything had narrowed down to getting through the day, to monitoring how I felt, to making sure I didn't spiral, to making sure I didn't have another attack, to making sure I stayed functional. Without realizing it, that became my entire focus, and everything else slowly faded into the background.

I didn't wake up one day and realize meaning was gone. I just noticed that life started to feel more about endurance than purpose, more about surviving than becoming something. And somewhere in that shift, without a clear moment or a clear reason, the version of me who believed life was building toward something meaningful started to disappear. I didn't know how to say that yet. I just knew I felt different, and whatever I had lost felt important, even if I couldn't name it. Once I started noticing that something was missing, I couldn't stop seeing it everywhere. It wasn't obvious at first, but it showed up in the way I thought about my life now compared to how I used to think about it before all of this started. Back then, even on hard days, I still had some kind of internal compass. I still believed I was moving forward, building something, becoming someone. Now it felt like I was just trying not to fall apart. I used to think about the future without fear. Not that I had everything planned, but there was this underlying belief that things would work out, that I would figure it out as I went. I had goals, even if they were messy. I had dreams, even if they weren't fully formed. There was meaning in trying. Now the future felt heavy. When I thought about what was ahead, my mind didn't go to possibility anymore. It went to anxiety. To exhaustion. To the quiet question of whether I'd feel okay enough to handle whatever came next.

Instead of asking myself what I wanted out of life, I was asking myself if I'd have the energy to get through it, And that hurt more than I expected it to. Because I didn't just lose motivation. I lost trust in myself. I stopped trusting that I could handle life the way I used to. Every plan came with a mental disclaimer, every idea was followed by what if you can't do this anymore, what if your anxiety gets worse, what if you have another attack, what if you can't keep up. That voice was always there in the background, quietly dismantling the future before it even had a chance to exist. I didn't realize how much space anxiety had taken up until I noticed how little room there was for anything else.

There wasn't much space left for dreaming or wanting or imagining. Most of my mental energy was being used just to stay regulated, to stay functional, to stay afloat. And when you're using that much energy just to feel okay, there isn't much left for building a life. That's when the grief really started to take shape, even if I still didn't call it that. It showed up when I thought about who I was supposed to be by now and felt like I had fallen behind in my own life. It showed up when I compared myself to people who seemed to be moving forward while I felt stuck managing my own head. It showed up in this quiet resentment that I didn't want to admit, resentment toward the fact that I had to spend so much time and energy just trying to feel normal. I didn't want to be doing this. I didn't choose this. I wanted my energy back. I wanted my curiosity back. I wanted the version of me who thought about the future with excitement instead of fear, who aspired that felt possible instead of overwhelming, who didn't wake up already wondering if today another day of managing symptoms would be.

Realizing that I missed that version of myself felt like losing someone I loved, not all at once, not cleanly, but slowly, quietly, and in pieces. The sadness didn't stay soft for long. At some point it started turning into anger, not the explosive kind, but the kind that sits in your chest and makes everything feel unfair. I didn't understand why this was happening to me, why my mind had changed in a way I didn't ask for, why something that felt so internal could take so much away from how I experienced my life. I remember thinking about how much effort it took just to feel okay and feeling bitter about it. Bitter that other people seemed to have space in their minds for dreams and goals and excitement while mine felt completely taken over by managing anxiety and trying not to spiral. Bitter that I had to think about things like whether I'd have another attack today while other people were planning trips or careers or futures without that constant background noise. It felt unfair that my energy was being spent on survival instead of growth. I didn't want to be strong. I didn't want to be resilient. I didn't want to "learn lessons" from this. I just wanted my old mental freedom back, the kind where I could think about what I wanted without immediately worrying about whether my body or my mind would cooperate. There were moments when I'd think about the life I imagined for myself before all of this and feel this sharp ache in my chest, like I was mourning a future that hadn't even happened yet.

I didn't know if I'd ever get back to that version of myself, and that uncertainty made everything feel fragile. Like I was rebuilding my life on ground that could shift at any moment. What made it harder was how invisible all of this was. No one could see what I was carrying. No one could see how much mental space was being taken up by fear and monitoring and self-management. From the outside, it probably looked like I was just tired or distracted or maybe even unmotivated, but inside it felt like I was fighting a quiet battle just to stay present. I didn't feel like myself anymore, but I also didn't know who I was becoming. That in-between space was uncomfortable and lonely. I wasn't the person I used to be, but I wasn't anything new yet either. I felt suspended between versions of myself, grieving one while not knowing what was supposed to replace them. And underneath all that anger and confusion was this deep fear that maybe the old me wasn't coming back. That maybe this wasn't just a phase or a detour, but a permanent shift.

That the person who lived with purpose and direction and excitement might be gone for good. I didn't say that fear out loud. I barely let myself think it all the way through. But it was there, shaping the way I saw everything, sitting quietly behind my thoughts, making the grief heavier because it wasn't just about what I had lost, it was about what I might never get back. I started comparing my life to what I thought it was supposed to look like by now, and that comparison never went well. It wasn't even about other people at first, it was about the version of myself I had imagined years ago, the one who would have things figured out, or at least feel like they were moving in the right direction. I used to picture a future where I was chasing goals, making plans, building something that felt meaningful. Now it felt like I was stuck maintaining myself instead of becoming anything new. Every time I thought about where I was, there was this quiet sense of being behind. Behind in life. Behind in growth. Behind in purpose.

Like time had kept moving but I had gotten stuck dealing with something that no one else could see. And the worst part was that it didn't feel like a temporary pause. It felt like an indefinite delay with no clear end point. I'd watch other people talk about their plans so easily, about what they wanted to do next, where they were headed, what they were excited about. And instead of feeling inspired, I felt tired. I felt disconnected from that version of life. My mind didn't work like that anymore. Every plan felt conditional. Every dream came with an asterisk. If my anxiety lets me. If I don't have another attack. If I feel okay enough. That constant "if" changed everything. It made me cautious in a way I never used to be. I stopped imagining big futures because imagining them hurt. It reminded me of how far I felt from the person I used to be, the one who didn't need to factor fear into every decision. I didn't stop dreaming because I didn't want to, I stopped because dreaming I felt unsafe. And there was a quiet grief in realizing that. Because ambition used to feel natural. Hope used to feel natural. Now they felt like risks.

Like things that could be taken away again. And when you've already lost a version of yourself without warning, it's hard to trust that anything is stable enough to build on. I didn't talk about this part much, even in my own head. It felt selfish to complain about being "behind" when I was still functioning, still showing up, still living. But that didn't change the fact that I felt disconnected from my own timeline. Like my life had split into a before and after, and I was still trying to figure out how to live in the after without constantly looking back. I missed the version of me who believed life was opening up instead of closing in. And admitting that hurt, because it meant acknowledging that something real had been lost, something I couldn't just back into existence by trying harder or thinking differently. It meant accepting that grief doesn't only come from losing people or moments. Sometimes it comes from losing momentum, direction, and the sense that your life is unfolding the way it's supposed to. That kind of grief is quiet, but it sits deep.

There was a point where the sadness and comparison turned into something heavier, something closer to resentment, and I didn't like admitting that to myself. I didn't want to feel bitter, but I was. Bitter that I had to rebuild myself in the middle of my own life, without choosing to, without understanding why this was happening in the first place. Bitter that so much of my energy was going toward fixing and managing and coping when all I really wanted was to live the way I used to. It felt unfair that I had to spend so much time thinking about my mental state when other people seemed free to just exist. I wasn't wishing bad things on anyone, but I couldn't stop thinking about how effortless life looked from the outside. How people talked about plans and goals like their minds were stable ground, like they didn't have to question whether they'd feel okay tomorrow or whether their anxiety would hijack their day.

I didn't want to be this careful version of myself. I didn't want to weigh every decision against how my body or my mind might react. I didn't want to think about exits, escape plans, or worst-case scenarios when all I was trying to do was live a normal day. And the fact that I had to do that now made me feel angry in a way that didn't have a place to go. What made it harder was knowing that no one had asked me to change, but I had changed anyway. I wasn't rebuilding because I wanted growth or self-improvement. I was rebuilding because I didn't have a choice. Something had broken, or shifted, or worn down inside me, and now I was responsible for putting the pieces back together without even knowing what the finished version was supposed to look like. That responsibility felt heavy. Some days it felt like I was starting from scratch, emotionally and mentally, while the world expected me to keep up like nothing had happened.

Like I was learning how to live again while pretending I already knew how. And that disconnect made me tired in a way that rest didn't fix, because it wasn't my body that was exhausted, it was the constant effort of adapting. I started to realize that grief isn't always about what's gone, it's about what you have to replace it with. About the work of becoming someone new when you weren't ready to let go of who you were. About the anger that comes with being forced into change before you've had a chance to make peace with the loss. And underneath all that resentment was a quieter fear that rebuilding might never fully bring me back to myself. That even if I learned how to cope, how to manage, how to survive, I might always miss the version of me who didn't have to think this hard just to exist. That fear didn't stop me from moving forward. But it did make every step feel heavier, like I was carrying both who I used to be and who I was becoming at the same time, and neither one felt like home yet. I think what hurt the most was realizing that the old version of me didn't just disappear, it slowly became unreachable.

Like I could still remember what it felt like to be them, but I couldn't step back into that feeling no matter how much I wanted to. It was like standing on one side of glass, close enough to see everything clearly but unable to cross back over. I'd try to do things the way I used to, thinking maybe if I acted like my old self, I'd start to feel like them again, but it never worked the way I hoped. I could go through the motions, say the right things, even feel brief flashes of familiarity, but underneath it all there was this constant awareness of my anxiety, this quiet tension that reminded me I wasn't the same anymore. And that realization came with its own kind of grief. Because it wasn't just that I missed who I was, it was that I couldn't rely on myself the way I used to. I used to trust my mind to handle things, to adapt, to push through without falling apart.

Now everything felt fragile. Like one wrong thought or one bad day could undo whatever stability I thought I had. That lack of trust changed how I moved through the world. I second-guessed myself more. I hesitated where I used to be confident. I held back where I used to lean in. And every time I noticed myself doing that, it felt like another small loss, another reminder that something fundamental had shifted. There was also this strange guilt that came with missing my old self, like I was being ungrateful for the person I was becoming. People talk a lot about growth and resilience and becoming stronger through struggle, but I didn't feel stronger. I felt tired. I felt like I was constantly adapting to a version of life I didn't choose. I didn't want to romanticize the past, and I knew logically that my old life wasn't perfect, but that didn't stop me from missing the simplicity of it. I missed waking up without immediately checking how I felt. I missed making plans without wondering if my anxiety would ruin them. I missed having mental space that wasn't constantly occupied by fear and self-monitoring.

That space mattered more than I realized at the time. Because without it, everything felt compressed. My thoughts, my emotions, my sense of self all felt crowded by this constant awareness of my mental state. And when you're living like that, it's hard to feel like yourself in any meaningful way. I didn't know how to grieve that loss properly. There was no ceremony for it, no clear moment of acceptance. It was just this ongoing ache, this quiet longing for a version of me who felt free in ways I hadn't appreciated until they were gone. And even though I didn't say it out loud, not to anyone else and barely to myself, part of me was terrified that I'd spend the rest of my life missing someone I used to be while trying to learn how to live as someone new. That thought sat with me longer than I wanted to admit.

There were moments when the grief would hit me out of nowhere, not in big emotional waves but in small realizations that caught me off guard. I'd be doing something normal, something simple, and suddenly notice how different it felt compared to how it used to, and that contrast would sink in hard. It could be something small, like planning my day or thinking about the week ahead and realizing that my first thought wasn't excitement or curiosity anymore, it was whether I'd feel okay enough to handle it. That's when it really started to hurt, because I could see how much my inner world had changed. Life used to feel like something I was moving toward, something I was actively participating in. Now it felt like something I was managing. Like my role had shifted from living to maintaining, from dreaming to monitoring. I wasn't asking myself what I wanted anymore, I was asking myself what I could handle, and that difference felt massive even though it looked small from the outside.

I didn't notice right away how much that mindset had taken over, but once I did, I couldn't ignore it. Every decision felt filtered through anxiety, through exhaustion, through the fear of setting myself up for failure or another spiral. Even things I wanted felt risky now, like wanting too much might make everything fall apart again. And there was grief in that restraint. Grief in holding myself back when I used to move forward without hesitation. Grief in watching my own ambition shrink, not because I didn't care, but because caring felt dangerous. I started protecting myself from disappointment before it even had a chance to exist, and in doing so, I slowly cut myself off from the parts of life that used to give me meaning. I didn't know how to talk about that loss without sounding dramatic or ungrateful, so I kept it to myself. I told myself this was just a phase, that once I got through whatever this was, I'd go back to being the person I used to be. But the longer it lasted, the harder it became to believe that was true.

There was this quiet fear underneath everything, the fear that the old me wasn't waiting on the other side of this, that maybe there was no "going back," only adapting and adjusting and learning how to live with a mind that no longer felt safe or predictable. That fear made the grief heavier, because it wasn't just about what I had lost, it was about the uncertainty of what I'd ever get back. I wasn't just missing who I was. I was missing who I thought I was becoming. And realizing that felt like losing my footing in my own life, like standing still while the version of the future I had imagined quietly slipped out of reach. I think one of the hardest things to accept was how much my identity had quietly shifted without my permission. I didn't wake up and decide to be someone who thought about anxiety every day, someone who measured their life in how manageable it felt instead of how meaningful it was. It just happened, slowly, while I was focused on getting through things, while I was telling myself this was temporary and I'd deal with it later. Before all of this, I used to define myself by what I wanted, by where I was headed, by the ideas I had about my future. There was a sense of movement in me, even when I wasn't sure what direction I was going.

Now when I tried to describe myself, my thoughts went to how I felt, how stable I was, how much energy I had, whether I was okay or not. My inner world had become the main event, and everything else felt secondary. That shift made me uncomfortable, because it felt like I was shrinking in ways no one else could see. I didn't like that my personality felt wrapped around my symptoms. I didn't like that so much of my mental space was taken up by managing myself instead of expressing myself. It felt like I had traded depth for safety, traded ambition for control, and even though I knew why it was happening, that didn't make it hurt less. There were moments when I'd try to reconnect with my old sense of purpose, like revisiting old goals or thinking about dreams I once had, and instead of feeling inspired, I'd feel overwhelmed or sad. Not because those things didn't matter anymore, but because they felt out of reach in a way they never had before. It was like looking at a life that belonged to someone else, someone I remembered being but didn't know how to become again.

I started to notice how often I introduced myself internally as someone who was "dealing with stuff" instead of someone who was building something. That realization stung, because it meant my identity had shifted from creator to caretaker, from dreamer to manager. I was spending so much energy keeping myself afloat that there was very little left to imagine what else I could be. And I didn't know how to grieve that properly.

There's no clear way to mourn a version of yourself who still technically exists, who still lives inside your memories, who still shows up in flashes when you least expect it. There's no ritual for that kind of loss, no language that feels big enough to hold it.

So, I carried it quietly, feeling the weight of it without fully understanding what I was holding. I wasn't just grieving who I used to be in the past. I was grieving the sense of direction I used to live with, the feeling that my life was unfolding with intention instead of being constantly redirected by fear and self-monitoring. And even though I kept telling myself that this wasn't the end of my story, that things could still change, that I was still here and still capable, there was a deep sadness in realizing that whatever came next would never be untouched by this experience. The old me lived in a world where anxiety wasn't a constant consideration. That world was gone. And accepting that felt like closing a door I never wanted to shut, even though I didn't yet know what was waiting on the other side.

What made the grief heavier was realizing that I couldn't talk about it the way people usually talk about loss. There was no clear thing to point to, no single moment or event that explained why I felt this way. I hadn't lost a person. I hadn't lost a job or a relationship or a place. I had lost a sense of myself, and that kind of loss is hard to justify, even to yourself. I'd think, how do you explain missing someone who is technically still you? I couldn't say, "I'm grieving," because it felt dramatic, like I was borrowing a word that belonged to bigger, more obvious pain. So instead, I stayed quiet and carried it internally, letting it show up in small ways. In the way I felt disconnected from my own life. In the way I felt sad when I thought about who I used to be, even if I couldn't explain exactly what I was sad about. There were times when I felt embarrassed by how much I missed that version of myself. Like I was being weak for wanting things to be easier again, for wanting my mind to feel safe and open and curious the way it used to. I'd tell myself I should be grateful, that I should focus on what I still had instead of what I lost, but that kind of thinking never really helped. It just added shame on top of grief. I wasn't wishing to go backward in time.

I wasn't trying to pretend nothing had happened. I just missed feeling grounded in myself. I missed waking up with a sense of purpose instead of a checklist of things to manage. I missed trusting my own thoughts without questioning whether they'd turn against me later in the day. And the more I tried to push that grief down, the more it showed up anyway. It showed up in quiet moments when I had time to think. It showed up when I saw glimpses of my old self in memories or conversations and felt that familiar ache in my chest. It showed up in this constant awareness that my life had changed in a way I didn't ask for, and no amount of pretending was going to undo that. I think part of what made it so painful was the feeling that I was grieving alone. Not because no one cared, but because I didn't know how to share something so abstract. It felt too internal, too personal, too complicated to put into words without worrying about being misunderstood.

So, I held it in. I carried the grief quietly, letting it sit in the background of my days, shaping the way I saw myself and my life. I didn't know yet how to let myself mourn without feeling guilty for it. I just knew that pretending I hadn't lost anything wasn't working. And that realization stayed with me, heavy and unresolved, waiting for me to eventually acknowledge that grief doesn't need permission to exist. It doesn't need a dramatic reason. Sometimes it just needs honesty, even if that honesty is uncomfortable and unfinished.

At some point, without really deciding to, I started realizing that holding onto the old version of myself as the only acceptable outcome was slowly hurting me. Not because missing them was wrong, but because I was measuring every day against a version of life that no longer existed in the same way. I kept comparing who I was now to who I used to be, and every comparison felt like proof that I was failing at something I didn't even choose. That realization didn't come with relief. It came with another layer of sadness, because it meant accepting that things had changed whether I liked it or not. I couldn't just wait to become who I used to be again. I couldn't put my life on pause until my mind felt the way it did before anxiety and depression took up so much space. Time was still moving, and I was still here, even if I didn't feel ready to be. I started to see how tightly I was clinging to the past, not because it was perfect, but because it felt safe. The old me didn't have to think this hard just to exist.

The old me didn't wake up already scanning their body and their thoughts for signs of trouble. The old me had room to want things without immediately worrying about whether they could handle them. Letting go of that version felt like giving up safety, even though that safety was already gone. And that's where the grief got complicated. Because I wasn't just sad about what I had lost. I feared what replacing it would mean. If I stopped hoping to return to who I was, then who was I supposed to become instead? What does it mean to build a life when your mind doesn't feel reliable anymore? What does meaning look like when so much of your energy is spent just trying to stay regulated and present? Those questions didn't have answers, and sitting with unanswered questions made everything feel unstable. But I started to realize that refusing to ask them wasn't protecting me either. It was keeping me stuck, holding my breath for a version of myself that might not come back in the way I wanted.

That didn't mean I was ready to let go. It just meant I was starting to understand that grief wasn't something I could rush through or ignore. It was something I had to carry while figuring out how to live alongside it. I could miss who I was and still exist as who I was becoming, even if that becoming felt unclear and unfinished. That idea didn't feel hopeful yet. It felt uncomfortable and uncertain. But it felt honest. And honesty, at that point, was the closest thing I had to solid ground. The thought that scared me the most wasn't that things were hard, it was the idea that meaning might be gone altogether and I just hadn't admitted it yet. Not hidden somewhere waiting for me to find it again, not delayed until I felt better, but gone, like it belonged to a version of me that no longer existed and couldn't be recovered in the way I wanted. I didn't think that thought all at once. It crept in slowly, in pieces, in moments where I noticed how empty my days felt even when they were full. I could get through a day and look back at it and feel nothing about it, no sense of progress, no feeling of purpose, no internal marker that said this mattered.

The day just happened, and then it was over, and then another one started. Before all of this, meaning didn't feel like something I had to chase. It was just there, woven into wanting things, planning things, believing I was moving toward something even if I didn't know exactly what that something was. Life felt like it was unfolding, and I was inside of it, participating in it. Now life felt flat. Not tragic. Not dramatic. Just empty in a way that made me uncomfortable. I started wondering what I was doing all of this for. Why I was pushing myself to wake up, to function, to keep going through days that felt heavy and dull and exhausting if there was nothing on the other side of it that felt meaningful anymore. I wasn't thinking about disappearing, but I was deeply unsettled by how hollow things could feel when the sense of direction disappeared. That scared me more than sadness ever did.

Sadness at least feels connected to something. It hurts because something mattered. But this felt like drifting, like floating without an anchor, like existing without a clear reason beyond the fact that time keeps moving and I'm still here inside it. And the more I noticed that feeling, the harder it became to ignore. I tried to convince myself that meaning would come back once I felt better that this emptiness was just a side effect of anxiety and depression, not something permanent. But the problem was that I didn't know what "feeling better" even meant anymore. I didn't know what I was working toward. I didn't know what version of myself I was waiting for. And that uncertainty made everything feel unstable. There were moments when I'd stop and think, is this really it right now? Is this all I'm doing, just managing myself day after day, trying to feel okay enough to get through things without building anything that feels like a life?

Every time that thought surfaced, I felt this tightness in my chest, like my body was reacting before my mind could soften it. I didn't want to think this way. I didn't want to question the point of things. I didn't want to sit with the possibility that meaning wasn't waiting for me in the future the way it used to feel like it was. So, I distracted myself. I stayed busy. I told myself not to spiral, not to go there, not to ask questions that didn't have answers. But the questions didn't go away. They showed up when things were quiet. When I was alone. When I finished something and realized I felt nothing about it. When I thought about the future and felt blank instead of hopeful. When I noticed how much of my energy was going toward not feeling worse instead of moving toward something better. And every time those moments happened, the grief felt heavier. Because it wasn't just grief for who I used to be anymore. It was grief for the sense that life had an underlying meaning I could trust. It was grief for the feeling that my effort was leading somewhere. Without that, everything started to feel fragile, like I was putting energy into days that didn't add up to anything solid.

I didn't say any of this out loud. I barely let myself think it all the way through. It felt too big, too uncomfortable, too close to questions I wasn't ready to answer. But it sat there anyway, underneath everything, shaping how I moved through my life even when I pretended it wasn't. I kept going, because stopping wasn't an option. But I was carrying this quiet fear with me, the fear that meaning wasn't just lost temporarily, but fundamentally altered, and that I might have to figure out how to live without the version of it I used to rely on. And I didn't know how to do that yet. I just knew that pretending everything was fine wasn't working, and neither was telling myself this feeling didn't matter. It mattered because it was there, because it kept coming back, because it changed the way everything else felt. I wasn't ready to accept it. I wasn't ready to understand it, but I couldn't ignore it anymore. What made that fear even heavier was the resentment that followed it, the quiet kind that doesn't explode but sits in your body and colors everything. I didn't want to be resentful, but I was. I resented the fact that I had to rebuild myself at all, that I had to think this hard about things that used to feel automatic, that my life had been interrupted by something I didn't invite and didn't understand.

I kept thinking about how unfair it felt to be handed this responsibility without consent. I didn't ask to learn coping skills. I didn't ask to become hyper-aware of my thoughts and my body. I didn't ask to spend my energy monitoring myself instead of living. And yet here I was, expected to adapt, expected to grow, expected to keep moving forward like this was just another challenge to overcome. People talk about rebuilding like it's empowering, like starting over is some clean slate moment where you get to choose who you become. But this didn't feel like a choice. It felt like being forced to reconstruct your life while still grieving the one you lost, without being given time to sit down and catch your breath. It felt like being told to move on when you hadn't even fully understood what had happened. I wasn't rebuilding because I wanted to be better. I was rebuilding because staying the same wasn't an option anymore. And that distinction mattered. Some days the resentment showed up as anger, other days as exhaustion, and sometimes as this deep resistance to the idea that I was supposed to find something positive in all of this. I didn't want to hear about lessons or silver linings. I didn't want to frame this as growth. I just wanted my life to feel like mine again, without having to constantly account for anxiety and fear. I remember feeling tired of being told, even indirectly, that this was part of becoming stronger. I didn't feel stronger. I felt worn down.

I felt like I was constantly compensating for something that had broken inside me, and no one could see how much effort that took. From the outside, it probably looked like I was still functioning, still showing up, still doing what I needed to do. But internally, it felt like I was rebuilding my foundation while still standing on it. There was also this resentment toward time itself. Toward the fact that days kept passing whether I felt ready or not. I didn't get to pause my life to grieve properly. Responsibilities didn't disappear just because I was struggling internally. I was expected to keep up, to keep producing, to keep being present, even while parts of me felt shattered and unfinished.

That pressure made the grief heavier. Because it wasn't just about loss anymore, it was about being forced to adapt before I had even accepted what I had lost. It was about learning new rules for living while still missing the old ones. And the more I tried to rush myself through that process, the more resentful I became, not just toward the situation, but toward myself. I didn't want to be this version of me. I didn't want to live inside this constant state of management and caution. I didn't want to build a life around my symptoms. And admitting that made me feel guilty, like I was rejecting the person I was becoming before I even knew them. But the truth was, I wasn't rejecting growth. I was rejecting the idea that this should be easy, or meaningful, or transformative right now. I was rejecting the pressure to turn pain into purpose before I had even allowed myself to feel the pain fully. I wasn't ready to rebuild. I was still grieving, and being forced to do both at the same time made everything feel heavier than it already was. I carried that resentment quietly, because I didn't know where else to put it. I didn't know how to express it without sounding ungrateful or negative or stuck. But it was there, shaping how I felt about myself and my life, reminding me that this wasn't a journey I chose, even if it was one, I was now stuck navigating. And the hardest part was knowing that whether I liked it or not, rebuilding was happening anyway, slowly, imperfectly, while I was still trying to come to terms with the fact that I shouldn't have had to rebuild at all.

What I missed the most, even more than the goals or the dreams or the version of myself that felt confident and capable, was the feeling of mental safety. I didn't realize how much I had relied on that before it was gone. Back then, my mind felt like a place I could live in without fear, a place where thoughts came and went without threatening to overwhelm me, a place that didn't constantly turn against itself. Now my mind felt unpredictable. I never knew when a thought would spiral into something bigger, when a normal feeling would suddenly feel dangerous, when my body would react before I even had time to understand what was happening. That constant unpredictability made me tense in a way that never fully went away. Even on "good" days, there was this background awareness that something could shift at any moment, and I hated living with that kind of vigilance. I missed trusting myself. I missed being able to think without immediately questioning my thoughts, without wondering if they were rational or anxiety-driven or the beginning of another spiral. I missed making decisions without scanning my body for signs of discomfort. I missed the ease of just existing inside my own head without feeling like I had to supervise it.

That loss was hard to explain, even to myself, because it wasn't something anyone else could see. On the outside, nothing looked different. Inside, it felt like I was living in a house where the floor could give out at any moment, and no matter how familiar the rooms were, I never felt fully at home anymore. I started to notice how careful I'd become with my own thoughts. I avoided certain topics. I shut down certain lines of thinking before they could go too far. I distracted myself constantly, not because I wanted to be entertained, but because silence felt risky. Too much quiet gave my mind room to wander, and I didn't trust where it might go. That constant self-monitoring was exhausting. It made me feel like I was always on guard, even with myself. And over time, that vigilance started to feel like another loss layered on top of everything else. I wasn't just grieving who I used to be or the future I had imagined, I was grieving the simple comfort of feeling safe inside my own thoughts. I remember moments where I'd catch myself longing for something as basic as mental calm, not happiness or excitement, just calm. The kind that lets you breathe without thinking about breathing, the kind that lets you sit still without wondering if something is wrong. And realizing how much I missed that made the grief sharper, because it reminded me of how far I felt from that state now.

There was also fear tied into that grief, fear that this sense of instability might be permanent. That maybe my mind would never feel fully safe again, that I'd always have to manage it, watch it, control it. The idea of living the rest of my life that way felt overwhelming, and I didn't know how to think about the future without that fear creeping in. I didn't want to believe that this was my new normal, but I also couldn't pretend it wasn't my current reality. And living in that tension, between hoping things would change and fearing they wouldn't, made the grief deeper and more complicated. Because I wasn't just mourning what I had lost. I was mourning the sense of security I used to take for granted. And losing that made everything else feel fragile, like even rebuilding myself would require learning how to live in a place that no longer felt entirely safe. I didn't realize how attached I had been to the future until it started slipping away from me. Not in a dramatic sense, not like a single plan fell apart, but in this quieter, more unsettling way where the life I assumed I was moving toward no longer felt reachable. It wasn't that I had specific milestones mapped out, it was the feeling that my life was opening, that time was something I could step into with curiosity instead of fear.

That feeling disappeared before I noticed it was gone. I used to think about the future like it was a place I'd eventually arrive at, a version of my life that made sense if I just kept moving. Even uncertainty felt okay back then, because it still carried possibility. I trusted that whatever came next would be something I could handle, something I could grow into. Now when I tried to think that far ahead, my mind stalled out. The future didn't feel like a place anymore, it felt like a question mark I didn't want to look at too closely. And that hurt more than I expected. Because it meant I wasn't just grieving who I used to be, I was grieving a life that never even got the chance to exist. The version of me who would have kept dreaming without fear, who would have chased goals without constantly checking in on their body, who would have moved forward without anxiety shaping every decision. That version of my future felt erased, replaced by something uncertain and fragile. I remember trying to imagine myself years from now and feeling blank. Not hopeful, not hopeless, just disconnected. Like the idea of "later" didn't belong to me anymore.

I could picture time passing, but I couldn't picture myself inside it with any clarity. And that scared me, because imagining a future used to be what gave my present meaning. Without that, days started to feel self-contained, like they didn't add up to anything bigger. I wasn't building toward something; I was just getting through. And while that was enough to survive, it wasn't enough to feel like my life was unfolding in a way that mattered. There was a quiet sadness in realizing that the life I thought I was going to have had been built on assumptions I could no longer make. I assumed my mind would be a stable place. I assumed fear wouldn't dictate my choices. I assumed challenges would be external, not internal. When those assumptions broke, the future I had imagined broke with them.

Grieving that kind of loss felt strange, because there was nothing tangible to mourn. No photos. No memories. Just a sense of what could have been, what should have been, what I thought I was moving toward without ever questioning it. That invisible loss sat heavy in my chest, even though I couldn't explain it to anyone else. I didn't want to accept that my future might look different now. I didn't want to let go of the version of life that felt easier, more expansive, freer. Letting go felt like giving up, like surrendering something important before I was ready. But holding on hurt too, because every time I thought about it, I was reminded of how far away it felt. So, I lived in that tension, caught between a future I missed and a future I couldn't imagine yet. Neither one felt solid. Neither one felt safe. And that made the grief linger, because it wasn't just about the past anymore, it was about the uncertainty of everything ahead. I wasn't just mourning what had been taken from me. I was mourning the life I thought I was walking toward. And learning how to sit with that loss, without rushing to replace it or explain it away, was one of the hardest parts of this whole experience.

I didn't reach some clear conclusion at the end of all this grief. There wasn't a moment where I decided to let go or accept what had happened or feel ready to move on. What I reached instead was a kind of stillness, not peaceful, not calm, just a pause where I stopped trying to force myself into an answer I didn't have. I was still grieving, still angry, and mostly still scared. But I was also tired of pretending that grief was something I could outthink or outgrow if I just tried hard enough. There were days when I woke up and immediately felt the weight of everything I had lost, not just the old version of me, but the ease, the safety, the future I had assumed was waiting for me. Other days it sat further back, quieter, but it never fully left. It followed me through normal moments, through conversations, through routines, reminding me that something fundamental had shifted and I didn't know yet how to live inside that shift.

I stopped trying to make the grief productive. I stopped asking what it was teaching me or how it was supposed to make me better. I didn't want lessons. I didn't want growth narratives. I just wanted permission to admit that losing who I was, and who I thought I would become, hurt more than I knew how to articulate. And the truth was, I didn't know how to replace that loss yet. I didn't know how to build meaning without the future I had imagined. I didn't know how to trust my mind enough to dream again. I didn't know how to live in a way that felt expansive when everything inside me felt cautious and contained. I was still trying to understand what kind of life was possible now, and every answer felt incomplete.

So I stayed in that unfinished place. I let myself miss the old me without trying to erase them. I let myself feel the grief without turning it into a problem that needed solving. I didn't forgive what had happened. I didn't make peace with it. I just acknowledged that this was where I was, standing between who I had been and who I might someday become, with no clear bridge between the two. That space was uncomfortable. It felt unstable and uncertain and lonely. But it was also honest. For the first time, I wasn't rushing myself toward acceptance or pretending I was further along than I was. I wasn't forcing meaning where there wasn't any yet. I was allowing the grief to exist without demanding that it transform into something useful. I didn't feel hopeful. I didn't feel resolved. I felt real. And at that point in my life, that was all I could manage. Being real about the loss. Being real about the fear.

Being real about not knowing what came next. I was still here, still breathing, still moving through days that felt heavy and unfinished, carrying the old me with me even as I stepped into a life that no longer looked the way I had imagined. I wasn't done mourning. I wasn't done changing. I was simply standing in the middle of it, learning how to exist without pretending that anything about this was simple or settled.

That's where Chapter Six ends.
Not with closure. Not with answers.
Just with honesty.

Chapter 7

Trying to Function – Work, relationships, and pretending

I didn't stop caring about the people in my life, but I slowly stopped letting them see me. Not intentionally, not in a way that felt cruel or deliberate, but in this quiet, almost invisible way where I started choosing what to show and what to keep buried so deeply that even I stopped checking on it. On the outside, I looked okay. Better than okay. I showed up. I talked. I laughed when I was supposed to. I kept conversations light, reassuring, normal. I learned how to answer questions in a way that shut them down gently without raising concern. I became good at saying I was fine in a tone that made people believe me. I did that because I didn't want to be a burden. I didn't want the people I loved, especially my family and my wife, to worry about me. I didn't want to add stress to their lives.

I didn't want to make them carry something I didn't even understand myself yet. So, I made a decision, without ever saying it out loud, that I would handle this on my own. I didn't realize at the time how isolating that choice would become. There were moments when people could tell something was off, when concern showed up in small ways, in questions that lingered a little longer than usual, in looks that felt searching instead of casual. And instead of letting that concern in, instead of using it as a chance to be honest, I pushed it away without even noticing I was doing it. I reassured everyone. I downplayed everything. I made it seem like nothing was wrong.

The more I did that, the more distance grew between how I felt and how I presented myself. I wasn't happy anymore, not in the way I used to be, but I didn't know how to say that without sounding ungrateful or dramatic or confusing. So I kept pretending. I kept performing the version of myself that people expected to see, even as the real version of me felt more exhausted and disconnected by the day. I didn't notice right away how much that pretending was costing me. It showed up in how quiet I became around the people closest to me, how I pulled back emotionally while still being physically present. I was there, but not really there. I listened, but with part of my mind somewhere else, constantly monitoring myself, constantly trying to keep everything together. And the worst part was that no one could really see it. They saw someone functioning. They saw someone stable. They saw someone handling life.

They didn't see how much effort it took just to maintain that image; how heavy it felt to carry everything alone while smiling through it. They didn't see how lonely it was to be surrounded by people who cared about you while feeling completely unseen. I told myself I was protecting them. I didn't realize I was slowly disappearing from my own life in the process. What hurt the most about my relationships wasn't conflict, it was the silence I created without realizing it. Especially with my family and my wife, the people who knew me best and loved me the hardest. I didn't stop loving them, not for a second, but I started filtering myself around them in ways that felt protective at first and slowly became isolating. I told myself I was doing the right thing by not worrying them. I convinced myself that keeping things light was a form of care, that if I stayed positive enough on the outside then maybe it would all stay manageable on the inside. I didn't want to be the reason the mood shifted. I didn't want conversations to revolve around me. I didn't want to turn normal moments into heavy ones.

So, I kept everything surface-level. I answered questions with half-truths. I shared updates without emotions. I talked about what I was doing, not how I was feeling. And over time, that became my default way of showing up, even with the people who deserved more honesty from me than anyone else. With my wife, it was especially complicated. She could sense that something was off, even when I tried my hardest to hide it. There were moments when she looked at me like she was searching for something, like she knew I wasn't fully there, and instead of letting myself be seen, I pulled back even more. Not because I didn't trust her, but because I didn't trust myself to explain what was happening without falling apart or making things worse. I didn't know how to say, I'm not okay, without feeling like I was failing in some way. Failing as a partner. Failing as someone who was supposed to be present, supportive, strong. I felt like admitting how bad things were inside me would somehow take something away from her, like my pain would become her burden, and I couldn't stand the thought of that.

So, I swallowed it. I stayed quiet when I should've spoken. I nodded when I should've opened up. I reassured when I should've admitted that reassurance was the one thing I didn't have for myself. And the more I did that, the more distance grew, not because love wasn't there, but because honesty wasn't. With my family, it felt similar but different. There was this unspoken pressure to be okay, to be the version of myself they recognized, the one who had things under control. I didn't want to worry them. I didn't want questions I couldn't answer. I didn't want to be watched with concern instead of trust. So, I showed up as the version of me that felt easiest for everyone else to accept. I didn't realize how lonely that would feel.

I could be in the same room, part of the same conversation, surrounded by people who cared deeply about me, and still feel completely alone inside my own head. Not because they didn't love me, but because they didn't know what was really going on, and I was actively keeping it that way. There were moments when concern did break through, when someone would ask a little more gently, a little more directly, and instead of letting that be an opening, I shut it down. I smiled. I reassured. I made it seem like everything was fine. And later, when I was alone, I'd feel this quiet ache knowing that I had just pushed away someone who was trying to reach me. But I didn't see it as pushing people away at the time. I saw it as protecting them. I saw it as handling things. I saw it as doing what I was supposed to do. I didn't realize that every time I chose to hide, I was also choosing to be alone with it. And that choice, repeated over and over again, started to shape my relationships in ways I didn't notice until much later.

Love was still there. Care was still there. But connection was thinning, stretched by silence and unspoken pain, and I didn't yet understand how much that pretending was costing both me and the people who loved me most. Work used to be one of the few places where I felt grounded. I loved my job, genuinely. It gave me structure, purpose, a sense that I was good at something and that what I did mattered. For a long time, work felt like a safe space, a place where I could focus, contribute, and feel like myself without having to think too much about everything else. That's why it was so unsettling when that started to change. At first, I told myself I was just tired. That everyone goes through phases where work feels heavier, where motivation dips a little. I didn't question it too much because I still showed up. I still did what I was supposed to do. I still met expectations. From the outside, nothing looked different, and that made it easier to convince myself that nothing *was* different. But inside, the joy was fading.

The things that used to excite me felt flat. The sense of pride I used to feel after a good day at work didn't land the same way anymore. I could accomplish something and immediately move on to the next thing without feeling anything about it. It wasn't that I stopped caring about my job, it was that caring felt harder to access, like it required energy I didn't have. Showing up started to feel mechanical. I'd go through the motions, complete tasks, have conversations, make decisions, all while feeling this quiet detachment underneath it all. I wasn't miserable at work, but I wasn't present either. I was there physically, doing my job well enough, but mentally I was often elsewhere, monitoring myself, checking in with how I felt, wondering if today another day would be I had to push through.

What scared me was how well I hid it. I became good at looking competent while feeling disconnected. I learned how to keep my voice steady, how to smile at the right times, how to stay engaged just enough that no one would question me. People trusted me. They relied on me. They saw someone who was handling things, someone who had it together, and every time that happened, I felt this strange mix of pride and sadness. Pride because I was still functioning. Sadness because no one could see how much effort that took. I remember moments where I'd sit at work and feel this quiet ache, realizing that something I loved no longer felt like a source of fulfillment, but just another place where I had to pretend.

I didn't dread work, but I didn't look forward to it either. It became another environment where I put on the same mask I wore everywhere else, the one that said I'm fine, I've got this, everything's okay. And I hated that. I hated that something meaningful to me had become another performance. I hated that even in a place where I once felt confident and capable, I now felt like I was just trying to get through the day without being exposed. I worried constantly about being found out, not because I was doing a bad job, but because I didn't feel like myself anymore, and I didn't know how long I could keep that hidden. There were moments when I'd catch myself thinking, if this doesn't make me feel anything anymore, what does that say about me? About my life? About how far this has gone? And those thoughts scared me, because work was one of the last places where I expected to feel this emptiness. Loving my job made it harder, not easier. Because I couldn't blame the work. I couldn't blame the environment. I couldn't say I was unhappy because of external factors. The problem wasn't out there. It was in me, and that realization followed me home at the end of every day, heavy and unresolved. I kept going because that's what I knew how to do. I showed up. I did my job.

I played my role. And every day I told myself I'd deal with how I felt later, when things slowed down, when I had more space, when I figured out what was wrong with me. But later never came. And slowly, quietly, the place that once gave me purpose became another place where I felt alone with what I was carrying, another reminder that I could be surrounded by people and responsibilities and still feel completely disconnected from my own life. Eventually everything started bleeding into everything else, and I couldn't keep the lines straight anymore. The pretending I did at work followed me home. The silence I carried at home followed me back to work. There was no place where I could fully take the mask off, no space where I felt like I could just exist without performing some version of okay. I started to feel like I was living two lives at the same time, and neither one felt real. On the outside, I was still showing up. I was still dependable. Still doing what needed to be done. Still answering questions, the way people expected me to. But inside, I felt like I was constantly holding my breath, waiting for the moment when I wouldn't be able to keep it together anymore.

Every interaction felt like a test I didn't know I was taking, every conversation another chance to accidentally reveal how far gone I felt. The exhaustion built slowly, not in my body at first, but in my mind. It was exhausting to remember what version of myself I had shown to which people. Exhausting to keep track of which feelings I had hidden and which ones I had minimized. Exhausting to constantly check myself before speaking, before reacting, before being honest. I wasn't lying outright, but I wasn't telling the truth either, and living in that in-between space took more energy than I realized. I remember moments where I'd be driving home after work and feel completely empty, like I had nothing left to give to anyone, not even myself. I'd walk through the door and immediately shift into another role, another version of me that was supposed to be present and engaged and fine. And some days I could pull it off.

Other days I felt like I was barely holding myself upright. What hurt the most was knowing how much love was around me and still feeling so alone inside it. My family cared. My wife cared. I could feel it in the way they checked in, in the way they paid attention, in the way concern would surface even when I tried to hide it. And instead of letting that care be a place to rest, it felt like pressure. Pressure to reassure them. Pressure to not make things worse. Pressure to stay strong even when I didn't feel strong at all. So, I kept choosing silence. Not because I didn't want support, but because I didn't know how to accept it without unraveling. I was afraid that if I started talking, I wouldn't know how to stop. Afraid that once I admitted how bad things felt, I'd confirm everyone's worst fears. Afraid that I'd become the thing I was trying so hard not to be, someone fragile, someone worrying, someone who needed too much.

I didn't see it then, but that fear was isolating me more than anything else ever could. There were nights when I'd sit next to my wife and feel this overwhelming urge to say something, anything, just to let her know how heavy everything felt. And instead, I'd stay quiet, telling myself I'd do it another time, when I had better words, when I felt more in control. That time never came. And each missed moment added another layer of distance I didn't know how to close. I started pulling away without meaning to. I became less expressive. Less open. Less available emotionally. Not because I didn't care, but because caring felt like something I didn't have the capacity for anymore. And the more I pulled back, the more disconnected I felt, creating this loop where loneliness fed the pretending and the pretending fed the loneliness. What scared me was how normal this started to feel. I got used to carrying everything internally. I got used to smiling through conversations. I got used to being "the one who's doing okay." And the longer I lived like that, the harder it became to imagine doing anything different.

This version of me, the functioning one, the quiet one, the composed one, slowly became my default, even though it felt nothing like who I really was. I didn't realize how much I was disappearing until I tried to remember the last time, I felt genuinely present in my own life, not just showing up, not just functioning, but actually there, and I couldn't remember. That realization didn't come with panic. It came with this dull, sinking feeling, like something important had slipped through my fingers while I was busy trying to keep everything together. I wasn't falling apart in obvious ways. I was just slowly fading into the background of my own life, prioritizing everyone else's comfort over my own truth. I told myself this was temporary. That I'd open when things calmed down. That I'd find the right moment to be honest. But deep down, I could feel how thin everything was stretched, how close I was to the edge of what I could carry alone. And still, I kept pretending. Because at that point, pretending felt safer than the risk of being seen.

The pretending started to feel less like a choice and more like a reflex, something my body did before my mind even had time to weigh in. I'd wake up already bracing myself, already preparing to step into the version of me that everyone recognized, the one who could handle things, the one who didn't make anyone uncomfortable with too much honesty or emotion. What I didn't realize was how much of myself I was leaving behind every time I did that. There were days when I'd catch a glimpse of myself in a quiet moment and feel this sharp awareness that I wasn't happy anymore, not in the way that used to come naturally. It wasn't constant sadness, it was more like a steady absence, like joy had slowly packed up and left without making a scene. Life kept going, but it didn't feel like it belonged to me the same way. And instead of talking about that, I buried it. I told myself it wasn't the right time. I told myself other people had enough going on. I told myself I didn't want to be the reason anyone worried or felt helpless.

So, I kept choosing silence, even when concern showed up in the people around me. Even when someone noticed I was quieter than usual, less present, less myself. I didn't notice right away how often I deflected. How quickly I changed the subject. How easily I minimized. How practiced I became at reassuring everyone else while feeling completely unsure inside. There were moments when I could tell my family sensed something was wrong, moments when questions came a little slower, a little softer, and instead of letting those moments open into honesty, I closed them down. I smiled. I shrugged. I said I was just tired. I made it seem manageable. And every time I did that, I felt this small ache afterward, knowing I had just pushed away someone who was trying to care for me. With my wife, that ache felt deeper. I could feel the distance growing even when neither of us talked about it. Not because love was missing, but because I was hiding in plain sight. I was right there, sitting next to her, sharing space, sharing routines, sharing a life, and still carrying this whole other reality inside me that I didn't know how to let her into. I wasn't trying to shut her out. I was trying to protect her. But protection turned into isolation faster than I understood.

There were nights when I lay there replaying conversations in my head, thinking about what I could have said, what I should have said, how close I came to opening up before stopping myself. I'd tell myself tomorrow would be different, that I'd find the right words, that I'd finally explain how heavy everything felt. And then tomorrow would come, and I'd put the mask back on without even thinking about it. The longer this went on, the more I started to feel like I was living a life no one else could see. I was present but unreachable. Loved but unseen. Surrounded but alone. And what hurt the most was knowing that this distance wasn't being created by anyone else. It was something I was building myself, piece by piece, in an attempt to keep everything from falling apart. I thought I was holding things together, but really, I was holding myself away from the people who might have been able to help carry some of the weight.

I didn't feel brave. I didn't feel strong. I felt tired of pretending, but too afraid to stop. And that fear kept me stuck in this in-between place, where I wasn't fully honest and I wasn't fully okay, where every day felt like another performance, I didn't know how to step out of without letting everyone down. I didn't realize yet that pretending, no matter how well-intentioned, was slowly eroding the very connections I was trying to protect. I just knew that each day felt heavier than the last, and that the version of me everyone saw was becoming harder and harder to maintain. There was a strange kind of pain in being told I was doing a good job, in being praised for how well I was handling things when handling things was the exact thing that was draining me. Every compliment felt like proof that my mask was working, and instead of feeling proud of that, it made me feel more alone. It meant no one could see how much effort it took just to stay upright, just to keep my voice steady, just to make it through the day without breaking down.

I'd hear things like you're so strong or you always handle things so well and something in me would sink a little every time. Not because those words were wrong, but because they were incomplete. They only reflected the version of me I was showing, not the version of me that went home exhausted from pretending, not the version that lay awake at night replaying everything I hadn't said, not the version that felt like it was constantly on the edge of being exposed. I started to feel trapped by that image of myself. Once people believed I was okay, it felt impossible to take that belief back. Admitting I wasn't okay felt like it would shock everyone, like it would rewrite the story they had already accepted about me. I worried that if I told the truth, people would feel blindsided, like I had been hiding something from them, which I guess I had, even though it never felt intentional. There was also this fear that if the mask slipped, even a little, everything would come out at once. That I wouldn't be able to explain it calmly or neatly.

That I'd cry or shut down or stumble over words and make everything feel heavier than I wanted it to be. I didn't trust myself to open the door just a crack. It felt like it was either completely closed or blown wide open, and both options scared me. So I kept it closed. I told myself it was safer that way, that I was sparing everyone discomfort, that I was being responsible. But inside, I felt this growing sense of loneliness that didn't make sense on paper. I wasn't isolated. I wasn't alone. I had people around me, people who cared deeply, and still I felt like I was carrying my life in secret. There were moments when I wanted someone to notice without me having to say anything, to see through the act and ask the right question in the right way. And then there were moments when someone did notice, when concern showed up uninvited, and I immediately shut it down. That contradiction lived inside me constantly, wanting to be seen and terrified of what being seen would mean. The pretending wasn't just exhausting, it was confusing. I didn't know where the act ended and I began anymore.

Some days I wondered if I was okay and just being dramatic in my own head. Other days I felt like I was barely holding it together and no one had any idea. That constant self-doubt made it even harder to speak up, because I couldn't trust my own perspective enough to defend it. I remember thinking that if I could just keep going a little longer, if I could just get through this phase, then maybe I'd figure it out on my own and no one would ever have to know how close I felt to the edge. I held onto that thought like a lifeline, even as the days blurred together and the weight didn't lift.

Being seen as strong started to feel like another burden I didn't know how to set down. I didn't want to disappoint anyone. I didn't want to change how people saw me. I didn't want to become a source of worry or concern. And somewhere in all of that, my own needs kept getting pushed further to the side, until I wasn't sure how to advocate for myself anymore. I wasn't falling apart loudly, I wasn't asking for help, I was quietly carrying everything, hoping that somehow, without anyone noticing, it would get lighter on its own, but it didn't. And the longer I pretended, the more I could feel how unsustainable it all was, how thin the line was between "functioning" and completely unraveling, even if no one else could see that line but me. There came a point where pretending stopped feeling sustainable, even if nothing had visibly fallen apart yet. From the outside, everything still looked the same. I was still showing up. Still doing what I needed to do.

Still playing the role I had been playing for a long time. But internally, something was cracking under the weight of it all. I started to feel it in my body before I could really name it in my mind. A constant tension that never fully relaxed. A heaviness that followed me everywhere, even into moments that were supposed to be calm. I could be sitting still and feel like I was bracing for something, like my system never got the message that it was safe to stand down. The pretending was no longer just tiring. It was draining me in a way that felt dangerous. I'd have moments where I felt disconnected from myself, like I was watching my life happen from a distance while trying to keep up appearances at the same time. Conversations felt harder to track. My patience wore thin more quickly. Small things overwhelmed me in ways that didn't make sense. And instead of seeing those as signs that I needed help, I treated them like personal failures I needed to hide better. I remember thinking, you're not even doing a good job at pretending anymore. That thought scared me. Because pretending was the only thing holding everything together.

It was the thing that allowed me to keep working, to keep showing up in my relationships, to keep life moving forward without drawing attention to how fragile I felt inside. The idea that I might lose even that ability made everything feel unstable. There were moments when I felt like I was one wrong question away from breaking. One genuine "are you okay?" asked at the wrong time could've undone me completely. And that fear made me even more guarded, even more careful, even more withdrawn, because I couldn't risk being seen when I didn't trust myself to stay composed. I started avoiding situations where I might be asked to be emotionally present. Not consciously, not in a dramatic way, but subtly. I stayed quieter. I kept conversations shallow. I limited how much of myself I gave to anyone, because giving anything felt like it might cost me more than I could afford. What hurt was realizing how much of my life was being shaped by that fear. I wasn't making choices based on what I wanted or what mattered to me.

I was making choices based on what felt safest for maintaining the act. What would require the least explanation. What would keep people from looking too closely. And living like that slowly stripped the life out of things, even the parts of my life I still cared deeply about. There were nights when I lay awake replaying the day, wondering how long I could keep this up, wondering what would happen if I couldn't. I didn't have a plan for what came next. I just knew that something about the way I was living wasn't working anymore, even if I didn't yet have the language to explain why. I wasn't ready to stop pretending, but I was starting to feel how close I was to the edge of what pretending could hold. And that awareness followed me everywhere, quiet but persistent, like a warning sign I didn't know how to respond to yet.

What made it harder was that nothing around me was giving me permission to stop. Life didn't slow down just because I was struggling internally. Work still expected me to show up. Relationships still expected me to be present. Responsibilities didn't pause to ask how I was really doing. And because everything kept moving, I kept moving too, even when I felt like I was being dragged along behind my own life. I remember feeling this quiet panic about how invisible my struggle had become, even to myself. I had spent so long pretending that I was okay that part of me started to believe it, at least enough to keep going. And then another part of me would surface, usually late at night or in moments of stillness, and remind me just how far from okay I really was. Living between those two parts felt disorienting, like I couldn't trust my own perception anymore. Some days I'd convince myself I was overreacting, that everyone feels this way sometimes, that this was just stress or exhaustion or adulthood. Other days I felt like I was barely holding myself together with sheer willpower alone. That constant swing made it even harder to reach out, because I didn't know which version of myself was the "real" one. I started to notice how often I was running on obligation instead of desire. I wasn't choosing things because I wanted to, I was choosing them because I felt like I had to. Because saying no felt like it would raise questions. Because slowing down felt like it would expose something I wasn't ready to talk about. Even rest started to feel performative, like I had to come back from it appearing refreshed, even if nothing inside me had actually changed.

There was this constant pressure to be okay enough, not great, not happy, just okay enough to keep everything from falling apart. And that pressure was exhausting in its own way. It meant there was no space to actually feel what I was feeling. No room to fall apart. No margin for honesty. Everything was about containment, about keeping things manageable, about staying within the lines of what was acceptable. I could feel myself becoming smaller inside that pressure. I wasn't expressing myself the way I used to. I wasn't reaching for connection the way I used to. I was conserving energy, rationing myself, trying to make sure I didn't spend too much in one place and have nothing left for the rest of the day.

Living like that made everything feel transactional, like I was constantly calculating how much of myself I could afford to give. What scared me was how normal that started to feel. I adapted to it. I adjusted my expectations. I accepted that this was just how things were now. And that quiet acceptance felt dangerous, because it meant I was slowly resigning myself to a life that felt flat and heavy and constrained, without ever actually choosing it. I wasn't collapsing, I wasn't asking for help, I was surviving in a way that didn't feel sustainable, and I didn't yet know how to stop. That realization didn't come with clarity or courage. It came with this dull awareness that something had to give eventually, even if I didn't know what that something was yet. And carrying that awareness while still pretending everything was fine made every day feel like walking on thin ice, careful and controlled and constantly aware of how easily things could break.

Eventually, the concern from other people started to feel louder, even though I was still doing everything I could to keep it from turning into something real. It showed up in small ways at first, in pauses that lasted a little too long, in questions that felt heavier than they sounded, in the way people looked at me like they were trying to read between the lines of what I was saying. And every time that happened, my instinct was the same, deflect, reassure, and minimize. I could feel people sensing that something wasn't right, especially the ones closest to me, and instead of feeling relieved that someone noticed, I felt exposed. Like the ground under my feet was thinning. I didn't want their concern to turn into worry, and I definitely didn't want worry to turn into questions I couldn't answer. So, I doubled down on pretending.

I became more convincing, more composed. I made sure my tone stayed even, my expressions stayed calm, my explanations stayed simple. I learned how to redirect conversations without making it obvious that I was avoiding something. I learned how to smile through moments that felt heavy and uncomfortable. And the better I got at it, the worse I felt afterward. Because every time someone reached toward me and I pushed them away, even gently, it left this quiet ache behind. There were moments with my wife where I could feel her concern sitting right there between us, unspoken but present, and instead of letting it turn into honesty, I pretended not to notice it. I acted normal. I acted steady. I acted like the version of myself she was used to seeing, even when I could tell that version didn't fully convince her anymore.

That scared me. Not because I didn't trust her, but because I didn't trust myself. I didn't trust that if I started talking, I'd be able to stop. I didn't trust that I could explain what was happening without it sounding worse than it already felt. I didn't trust that I could hold myself together if I let the truth surface. So I stayed quiet, even when silence made things heavier. With my family, it felt similar but layered with guilt. I could tell they noticed the changes. The quieter version of me. The distance. The way I didn't seem as present or engaged. And every time I reassured them that I was fine, a part of me knew I was lying by omission. Not because I wanted to deceive them, but because I didn't know how to be honest without causing pain. I didn't want to be the reason anyone worried. I didn't want to be the source of stress. I didn't want to change the dynamic of our relationships. So, I chose the version of honesty that felt safest for everyone else, even if it meant being unsafe with myself.

The problem was that the cracks didn't stop forming just because I tried harder. I started slipping in small ways. I'd lose focus mid-conversation. I'd seem distant when I should've been present. I'd get overwhelmed by things that never used to bother me. And every time that happened, I'd feel this rush of fear, like I was getting closer to being found out. I wasn't ready for that. I wasn't ready to explain myself. I wasn't ready to admit how bad things felt. I wasn't ready to let the version of me everyone trusted disappears. So I kept pretending, even as it got harder to maintain, even as it started to cost me more than it ever had before. The concern around me grew quieter but heavier, like people were waiting for something I wasn't giving them, and that tension sat in every interaction, whether anyone acknowledged it or not. I didn't feel relieved when people backed off. I felt lonely. Because what I really wanted was to be seen without having to explain myself, to be understood without having to expose everything all at once. But I didn't know how to create that kind of moment, and I didn't trust myself to survive it if it happened. So, I stayed in control. I stayed composed. I stayed silent. And the cost of that silence kept adding up, quietly, invisibly, until pretending no longer felt like something I was choosing, but something I was trapped inside.

There was no dramatic moment where everything collapsed. No single day I could point to and say, this is when it all fell apart. What happened instead was quieter and somehow more unsettling. I started to realize that I couldn't keep living like this, even though, technically, I still was. It came in small thoughts that wouldn't leave me alone. Thoughts like, how long do you think you can keep this up? or what happens if nothing changes? I wasn't panicking in those moments. I wasn't spiraling. I was just noticing, with this uncomfortable clarity, that the way I was functioning wasn't sustainable, and pretending otherwise wasn't making it any less true. I'd get through a day and feel completely empty afterward, like I had spent every ounce of energy just maintaining the version of myself everyone expected. There was nothing left at the end of it. No relief. No sense of accomplishment. Just this quiet awareness that tomorrow I'd have to do it all over again. And that thought felt heavy. I remember sitting in stillness, maybe late at night or early in the morning, and realizing how much of my life had become about endurance. Getting through. Holding it together.

Making sure nothing spilled over. I wasn't living toward anything. I was just surviving inside routines that felt increasingly hollow, and the idea of doing that indefinitely made something in me recoil. Not dramatically. Not with panic. Just with this deep internal resistance that said, this can't be it. I didn't want my life to be defined by how well I could hide my pain. I didn't want my relationships to be built on half-truths and reassurances. I didn't want my job, something I genuinely loved; to feel like another place I had to perform just to get through the day. And yet, that's exactly what my life had become. What scared me was how easy it would've been to keep going like that. Nothing was forcing me to stop. No one was demanding honesty. No crisis was pushing me to change. I could have continued pretending for a long time, maybe forever, and that possibility frightened me more than the idea of things falling apart. Because it meant I could slowly disappear from my own life without anyone ever noticing.

There were moments when I'd look at the people around me, especially my wife and my family, and feel this ache knowing how close I was to them physically and how far away I felt emotionally. I didn't want that distance to become permanent. I didn't want to look back one day and realize I had spent years being present in name only, too afraid to be real, too tired to be honest. But knowing that and acting on it felt like two very different things. I didn't suddenly find the courage to open. I didn't wake up ready to tell the truth. What I felt instead was this internal tension, like something inside me was pressing up against the walls I had built, testing them, reminding me they couldn't hold forever. That awareness followed me everywhere. At work. At home. In conversations. In quiet moments alone. It didn't demand action yet, but it refused to be ignored. It sat there, steady and persistent, telling me that pretending had taken me as far as it could, and that continuing down this path would cost me more than I was willing to pay.

I wasn't ready to stop functioning. I wasn't ready to ask for help. But I was starting to understand that something had to change, even if I didn't yet know what that change would look like. And that understanding marked a shift. Not a breakthrough. Not a turning point. Just the moment where I could no longer lie to myself about how unsustainable my life had become. Once that realization settled in, that I couldn't keep living like this, it didn't push me forward the way people like to talk about realizations. It didn't motivate me or energize me or make anything clearer. If anything, it made me more afraid, because now I could see the truth and still didn't know what to do with it. Change felt dangerous. Not because I didn't want things to be different, but because I didn't know what changing would cost me.

I didn't know how to stop pretending without everything unraveling at once. I didn't know how to be honest without becoming someone people worried about, someone fragile, someone who needed more than I felt allowed to need. So, I stayed in this strange holding pattern. Aware enough to know I was struggling. Not ready enough to do anything about it. That in-between space was suffocating. It felt like standing in a doorway without stepping forward or backward, knowing that either direction would hurt in its own way. If I stayed where I was, I'd keep disappearing. If I moved, I risked breaking the life I had worked so hard to keep intact.

I remember feeling this constant internal negotiation. Telling myself maybe I just needed more rest, more time, more patience. Maybe if I waited long enough, things would ease on their own and I wouldn't have to make any hard choices. That hope kept me stuck longer than I realized, because it gave me permission to delay without changing anything, But the weight didn't lift. It stayed with me in conversations where I felt myself holding back words that wanted to come out. It stayed with me at work, where the gap between how I looked and how I felt kept widening. It stayed with me at home, especially in the quiet moments, when there was nothing to distract me from the truth that I wasn't okay and hadn't been for a long time. I started noticing how often I felt tense even when nothing was happening.

How my body stayed on edge, like it was waiting for something I couldn't name. How relief never fully came, even on good days. And the more I noticed that the harder it became to believe that pretending was protecting me. It wasn't protecting me anymore. It was trapping me. Still, the idea of letting the mask slip felt overwhelming. I didn't know how to explain myself without sounding broken. I didn't know how to start a conversation that felt this big. I didn't know how to ask for help when I had spent so long convincing everyone, including myself, that I didn't need it.

So, I stayed quiet, even as the awareness pressed closer and closer to the surface. I wasn't ready to change yet, but I was no longer comfortable staying the same. And living inside that tension made every day feel heavier, like I was carrying not just my pain, but the fear of what acknowledging it might lead to. I kept functioning. I kept pretending. But now there was this constant, undeniable knowing underneath it all. Something had to give. Even though I didn't yet know how or when, I could feel that I was approaching the limits of what I could carry on my own. That knowing didn't make me brave.

It made me cautious in a new way. I started moving through my days like I was carrying something fragile, something that could shatter if I handled it wrong, and that something was me. Every interaction felt heavier because now I was aware of how close I felt to the edge of what I could manage, even if no one else could see it.I became more careful with my words. More careful with my reactions. More careful with how much of myself I revealed in any given moment. I wasn't just pretending anymore, I was controlling, constantly adjusting myself so nothing slipped out unintentionally. It felt like walking on uneven ground while pretending the path was flat, always watching my step, always afraid of losing my balance. There were moments when I wanted to say something honest, something simple like I'm not doing great lately, and even that felt like too much. I'd play the conversation out in my head, imagining the concern on people's faces, the follow-up questions, the worry that would settle in their voices. And instead of feeling relief at the thought of being seen, I felt panic. Panic at the idea of opening a door I didn't know how to close again.

So, I stayed silent. I convinced myself that staying quiet was the responsible choice, that I was protecting my family, protecting my wife, protecting the structure of my life. I told myself that if I could just hold it together a little longer, I'd figure it out on my own and spare everyone the mess of watching me struggle. That belief kept me going, even as it isolated me further from the people who cared most. What hurt was realizing how much love I was pushing away in the process. Not intentionally. Not maliciously. But by keeping myself hidden, I was also keeping others at a distance. I could feel it in the way conversations felt less connected, in the way emotional moments passed without me fully participating, in the way I'd nod and listen while feeling completely detached inside. I was there, but not available, and that disconnect made me feel like I was slowly losing my place in my own relationships. With my love, the guilt of that distance weighed on me constantly. I could feel how much she wanted to understand, how much she wanted to help, and my inability to let her in felt like a betrayal of the partnership we shared. I didn't want to shut her out, but I didn't know how to invite her in without unraveling myself in the process. That fear kept me stuck. I started to feel like I was living in this narrow emotional space where everything was about containment. Don't feel too much. Don't say too much.

Don't risk breaking the illusion. And living like that made everything feel smaller, tighter, more constrained. Even moments that should have felt comforting felt distant, like I was watching my life through glass. There were nights when I lay awake, staring at the ceiling, feeling the weight of everything I hadn't said pressing down on me. I'd replay the day, thinking about moments where I could have been honest and chose not to be, moments where I could have reached out and didn't. And with each missed opportunity, the sense of isolation deepened. I didn't feel strong for carrying it alone, I felt tired of carrying it at all. And yet, even with that exhaustion, I didn't know how to stop. The idea of continuing like this felt unbearable, but the idea of changing felt just as frightening. I was trapped between endurance and honesty, between keeping things together and letting things fall apart, and I didn't know which option would hurt less. So I stayed in that suspended place, aware of my limits, afraid of crossing them, still functioning on the outside while everything inside me felt stretched thin. I hadn't broken yet, but I could feel how close I was to something giving way, and that awareness sat heavy in my chest every single day. I was still pretending, still surviving. But now, pretending felt like it was costing me more than it was protecting me, and I didn't know how much longer I could keep paying that price.

There were moments when the mask slipped, not in front of anyone else, but inside me, in the quiet spaces where I couldn't keep up the act even for myself. It usually happened when I was alone, when there was nothing demanding my attention and no one watching to make sure I stayed composed. In those moments, the effort it took to function finally caught up with me. I'd feel this sudden wave of exhaustion, deeper than tired, heavier than stress, like my body and mind were both asking the same question at the same time: how much longer do you think you can do this? And I wouldn't have an answer. I'd just sit with that feeling, letting it wash over me, knowing I'd have to pull myself together again soon, knowing I couldn't stay in that honesty for very long. Those moments scared me, not because they were dramatic, but because they felt real in a way nothing else did. There was no pretending there. No reassuring tone. No version of me that was managing things well. Just the truth, raw and uncomfortable, that I was not okay and hadn't been for a while. Sometimes I'd imagine what it would be like to stop pretending completely. To tell my wife the full truth. To sit with my family and say I'm struggling, and I don't know why and I don't know how to fix it. And every time I let myself imagine that my chest would tighten. Not with relief, but with fear, fear of being seen as weak, fear of being a burden, and fear of changing how people saw me forever.

I worried about what honesty would do to my relationships. Would it worry them constantly? Would it change the way they treated me? Would it make me feel smaller instead of supported? I didn't know, and that uncertainty kept me frozen. It felt safer to keep everything contained inside me, even though that containment was slowly wearing me down. There was also this strange grief tied into the idea of being honest. Grief for the version of myself who didn't need to have these conversations, who didn't need to explain their mental state, who could just exist without turning their inner world into something that needed managing or discussing. Admitting I wasn't okay felt like admitting that version of me was really gone. I wasn't ready to face that yet. So when those honest moments passed, I put the mask back on and stepped back into my life like nothing had happened. I went back to functioning, back to reassuring, back to being the version of myself everyone recognized. And each time I did that, it felt a little heavier, like I was stacking weight on top of weight without ever setting anything down. The truth was, I didn't want to keep pretending, but I didn't know how to stop without everything changing. And that fear kept me stuck, oscillating between moments of clarity and long stretches of denial, never staying in either place long enough to move forward. I didn't feel ready to break.

I didn't feel ready to heal. I just felt caught. And living in that caught place, knowing something needed to change but not knowing how to make that change, made every day feel like a balancing act I was one misstep away from failing, even if no one else could see how unsteady I felt. I started rehearsing honesty in my head long before I ever let it come close to my mouth. I'd imagine sitting down with my wife, or with my family, and finally saying what I had been carrying for so long. I'd picture the words forming, simple and direct, nothing dramatic, just the truth. I'm not okay. I haven't been okay. I don't know how to fix it. And every time I imagined it, my body reacted before my mind could finish the thought. My chest would tighten. My breathing would change. My thoughts would scatter. It felt like opening that door would release something I wouldn't be able to contain, like once I admitted it out loud, there would be no way to put it back where it came from. I wouldn't just be telling them how I felt.

I'd be changing the reality we were all living in. That scared me. Because pretending, as exhausting as it was, still felt controlled. I knew how to do it. I knew how to manage people's expectations. I knew how to keep things moving. Honesty felt unpredictable. I didn't know how people would respond. I didn't know how much they'd want to know. I didn't know if I could handle their reactions on top of everything else I was already carrying. I worried that once I said it, everything would change in ways I wasn't ready for. That I'd be looked at differently. That concern would replace trust. That I'd become fragile in their eyes, even if I didn't feel fragile in the way people imagine. I didn't want to be handled carefully. I didn't want to be watched. I didn't want my every mood to be monitored. I just wanted relief. But I didn't know how to ask for relief without asking for everything else that came with it. There were moments when I could feel myself getting closer to saying something, when the weight inside me felt so heavy that staying quiet felt impossible. And then something would pull me back, a glance, a comment, a moment that reminded me how normal everything looked on the outside. I'd think, maybe I can get through another day. Maybe I can hold it together a little longer.

So, I did. I kept pushing the moment off. Tomorrow. Next week. When I have the right words. When I feel more in control. When I'm sure this isn't just a phase. And with every delay, the pressure inside me built, quietly, steadily, like something winding tighter and tighter. I started to sense that this wasn't going to stay contained forever. Not in a dramatic, explosive way. But in the way things break when they're under too much strain for too long. Slowly. Silently. Without warning. I could feel that I was approaching some kind of threshold, even if I didn't know what crossing it would look like yet. That awareness followed me everywhere. At work. At home. In conversations that felt normal on the surface but heavy underneath. I was constantly aware of how close I felt to saying something I couldn't take back, and that awareness made me even more guarded, even more careful. I didn't know how to prepare for what was coming. I just knew that pretending was no longer something I could do indefinitely, and that whatever came next would change something, whether I was ready for it or not. I was standing on the edge of honesty, afraid to step forward, afraid to step back, feeling the ground beneath me grow less stable with every day that passed. And deep down, even though I wasn't ready to admit it yet, I knew I was running out of space to keep everything hidden. Nothing actually changed yet. That was the strangest part.

There was no confession, no breakdown, no moment where everything finally spilled out. On the surface, life kept moving exactly the same way it always had. I still went to work. I still showed up at home. I still played my role. If someone had been watching from the outside, they wouldn't have noticed anything different. But inside, something had shifted. I could feel it in the way pretending no longer felt automatic. It took more effort now. More awareness. More energy. Every time I reassured someone that I was fine, there was this brief pause inside me, like a part of me hesitated before going along with it. Not because I suddenly wanted to tell the truth, but because I could feel how close I was to not being able to keep lying, even gently. I wasn't okay, and I knew it. That knowing sat with me constantly. It followed me through conversations, through routines, through quiet moments where I used to distract myself enough not to think too deeply. Now, no matter what I did, there was this underlying awareness that the way I was living couldn't continue forever. Not like this. Not in silence. Not while slowly disappearing from my own life. I felt torn between two instincts that pulled at me in opposite directions. One wanted to keep protecting everyone else, to stay strong, to avoid becoming a source of worry or concern.

The other wanted relief. Not dramatic relief. Not a solution. Just the relief of not having to pretend every single day. And I didn't know which instinct would win. I remember feeling this deep sadness, not sharp or overwhelming, but steady and heavy, realizing how much of myself I had pushed aside in the name of being okay for other people. I had prioritized comfort, stability, normalcy, even when it came at the cost of my own honesty. I had convinced myself that endurance was the same as strength, even as it hollowed me out. I wasn't angry anymore. I wasn't panicking. I was tired. Tired of carrying everything alone. Tired of monitoring myself. Tired of being praised for handling things I was barely surviving. And even though I still didn't know how to stop, I could feel that pretending was reaching its limit.

The space I had built to contain everything was shrinking. The weight inside me was pressing closer to the surface. Something was going to change, not because I was ready, but because I wouldn't be able to keep it hidden much longer. I didn't know what that change would look like yet. I didn't know how or when it would happen. I just knew that I was standing at the end of what pretending could give me. Whatever came next would require more honesty than I had allowed myself so far, whether I wanted it to or not. And that realization marked the end of this chapter of my life.

Not because anything had resolved, not because I had found answers, but because I could finally admit, even if only to myself, that the version of me who survived by pretending was running out of strength.

Chapter 8

Hitting Bottom – The moment I couldn't ignore it anymore

It doesn't feel like a collapse, It feels like a shift I can't name at first, like something in me quietly changes its shape while I'm still trying to treat it like the same old thing. Anxiety has been loud. Depression has been heavy. I've learned how to live around both in this weird way where I'm always adjusting, always checking myself, always trying to keep my life moving even when my mind is dragging behind me. But now there's something else sitting underneath it, something colder, something that doesn't come with the same panic or the same fog, something that feels too still. The thoughts start showing up more often than I want to admit. Not like lightning, not like a sudden scary image that flashes and disappears.

They show up like background noise that keeps turning the volume up, like a channel I never asked to tune into but somehow can't shut off. At first, I catch them and push them away, I tell myself they're intrusive, they don't mean anything, they're not me, they're just part of being overwhelmed. But they keep returning, and what scares me isn't just that they're there, it's how familiar they start to feel, like my mind is practicing them, like it's testing how it feels to think them and letting them linger a little longer each time. It isn't even death that my mind is obsessed with. It's silence. The idea of nothing. The idea of not having to manage anything anymore, not having to wake up and immediately start negotiating with my own head, not having to monitor my body for signs of panic, not having to force myself through another day while pretending I'm okay enough to be around people. I'm tired in a way that doesn't feel like sleep could fix it. I'm tired in a way that makes everything feel like effort, including being alive, including being present, including being the version of myself that has to keep trying.

I keep telling myself I'm fine. I keep telling myself I don't actually want to die, that I'd never do anything, that I'm not that kind of person, that this is just my brain being dramatic. I hold onto that like it's proof that I'm still in control. But the thought doesn't need me to want it. It doesn't need my permission. It's there anyway, circling, waiting for the moment I'm too exhausted to fight it. And I hate myself for how it even starts to sound appealing, not in a desperate, crying kind of way, but in a quiet, logical way, like my brain is offering it as a solution, like it's saying, you could stop all of this, you could let go, you could finally rest. That thought scares me more than panic ever has. Panic is terrifying, but it still feels like my body screaming. This feels like my mind whispering. This feels like something that could blend into my normal thoughts if I'm not careful, like something that could become a habit, like something that could become my default. I'm still doing life on the outside.

I'm still showing up. Still going through motions. Still functioning enough that no one would think I'm in danger. But inside, there's this quiet awareness that something has changed, like I've crossed into a place I never thought I'd enter, a place where the question isn't just how I get through today, it's why I even have to. I don't say any of this out loud. I don't even fully admit it to myself in a clean way. I just feel it. I carry it. I notice it in the spaces between things, in the moments when I'm alone and the mask isn't being worn for anyone, in the seconds when my brain gets too quiet and then fills the quiet with that same thought again. I can't live like this. It isn't a dramatic statement. It isn't an announcement. It lands inside me like a fact, like my body recognizes it before my mind wants to. And the scariest part is that I don't know what comes after that sentence. The thoughts don't arrive like an emergency.

They arrive like routine. That's what unsettles me most. They slide into my mind the way reminders do, the way unfinished tasks linger at the edge of attention, not demanding anything, just existing there, waiting to be acknowledged. I notice how easily they take up space, how little resistance they meet after a while.

At first, I argue with them. I tell myself they're intrusive, that they don't belong to me, that they're just a symptom passing through. I remind myself of everything I still have, everything I still care about, all the reasons this shouldn't be happening. But the reminders feel thin, like they're made of paper, and the thoughts feel solid, like they're made of something heavier. They don't shout. They don't threaten. They just sit there, calm and persistent, returning every time my mind goes quiet, every time I stop actively distracting myself. I start to realize how often I'm distracting myself; how much effort goes into keeping my attention busy just so those thoughts don't have room to settle in. And when they do settle in, they don't feel like a crisis. They feel like a suggestion. That's the part that scares me. It's not about wanting to be gone. It's about wanting the work of staying to stop. The constant monitoring. The effort it takes to be inside my own head. The way every day feels like a negotiation with myself that never fully ends.

The thought offers an end to all of that, not violently, not dramatically, just quietly, like closing a door and finally getting some rest. I catch myself thinking about relief more than anything else. Relief from thinking. Relief from trying. Relief from carrying this invisible weight that no one else can see. And when I notice that shift, when I realize that relief is starting to feel tempting, a cold fear moves through me. Because I know I'm not supposed to think this way. I know there's a line somewhere that I'm getting close to, even if I haven't crossed it yet. I tell myself I'm still safe because I haven't done anything, because I wouldn't do anything, because I still know better. But knowing better doesn't make the thoughts stop. It doesn't push them out. It just makes me more aware of how present they are. They show up in the middle of normal moments. While I'm doing something familiar. While I'm supposed to be relaxed. While nothing is technically wrong. That's when I start to understand how deep this goes, how this isn't just about stress or exhaustion anymore. This is something that's woven itself into the background of my mind. I start paying attention to how often the sentence repeats itself. I can't live like this. Not yelled. Not cried. Just stated. It sits there like a conclusion I didn't mean to reach but can't ignore once it's formed. I try to soften it, try to add conditions to it, try to tell myself it's just a moment, just a phase, just my brain being dramatic. But the sentence doesn't disappear when I argue with it. It just waits. I feel ashamed for how steady it feels. Ashamed that it isn't chaotic or emotional or obviously wrong.

Ashamed that it doesn't come with the kind of distress I've been taught to recognize as dangerous. This feels more dangerous because it feels reasonable, because it doesn't demand anything from me except acknowledgement. I keep functioning. I keep moving. I keep doing what I'm supposed to do. On the outside, nothing has changed enough to raise alarms. Inside, everything feels different. It feels like my mind has opened a door I don't know how to close, and now I'm aware of a way out that I never wanted to see. I don't want to go anywhere; I just want this to stop. And the more often that thought returns, the more I realize how little space there is between thinking it and believing it, how thin the barrier feels between surviving and surrendering, even if I'm still standing on the surviving side for now.

The distinction becomes clearer the longer I sit with it. I don't want to die. That sentence still feels true when I say it to myself, still feels like something I can hold onto. But right next to it lives another truth that's harder to admit, one that doesn't cancel the first one out, just complicates it in a way that makes everything heavier. I want everything to stop. Not life itself, not in the way people imagine when they hear those words. I want the noise to stop. The constant awareness. The endless self-monitoring. The feeling that I have to keep myself together every second of every day or risk everything unraveling. I want a break from my own mind, from the responsibility of staying okay enough to function, from the effort it takes just to exist. It feels important to be honest about that difference, even if it scares me. Because the thought doesn't come with violence or urgency. It comes with exhaustion. It comes with this deep longing for rest that goes beyond sleep, beyond time off, beyond anything I know how to give myself. It feels like my system is worn down from being on high alert for too long, like it's looking for the fastest way to shut everything off.

That's the part that makes me uncomfortable. If the thoughts were dramatic, if they came with panic or desperation, I'd know how to respond to them. I've dealt with panic. I know how to survive that. This is quieter. This feels like my mind is trying to solve a problem by removing itself from the equation, and the calmness of that idea is what makes my stomach drop. I catch myself thinking about what it would be like not to have to wake up and immediately assess how I feel. Not to have to brace myself for the day. Not to have to push through moments that feel heavier than they should. The appeal isn't in being gone. It's in not having to keep going like this. And then guilt follows. Guilt for even thinking this way. Guilt for not being stronger. Guilt for wanting relief instead of resilience. I tell myself other people have it worse. I tell myself I should be grateful. I tell myself this is temporary, that I'll figure it out, that I just need to hold on a little longer. But those thoughts feel like obligations more than comfort, like things I'm supposed to believe rather than things that help.

The truth is, holding on feels harder than letting go of the idea of holding on. That realization scares me enough to pull me back for a moment, to remind me that this is serious, that I'm in territory I never wanted to explore. I don't feel out of control, but I do feel close to something I don't understand yet, like I'm standing near an edge I didn't know was there until I was already too close to it. I try to ground myself. I try to focus on what's real, what's around me, what I can see and touch and feel. Sometimes that helps. Sometimes it doesn't. Sometimes the thoughts fade into the background. Sometimes they sit right there, quiet and patient, waiting for the next moment of stillness. I keep telling myself that wanting it to stop isn't the same as wanting to die. But I also know how thin that line can feel when you're exhausted enough, when relief starts to sound like an answer instead of an escape. I don't want to cross that line. I don't plan to. I just hate how often I find myself standing near it, looking at it, aware of it in a way I never have been before. This isn't a moment, It's a state. And the longer I stay in it, the more I realize how much energy it takes just to keep reminding myself that I want to stay, even when staying feels like the hardest thing I've ever done.

What unsettles me most is how calm everything feels when the thoughts settle in. I'm used to fear announcing itself loudly, with panic and racing thoughts and a body that won't cooperate. I know how to recognize that kind of danger. This doesn't feel like that. This feels steady. Measured. Almost reasonable. And that makes it harder to trust myself. The calm doesn't bring relief, it brings confusion. It makes me question whether I'm overreacting, whether this is as serious as it feels, because shouldn't something this dark come with more chaos? Shouldn't I feel frantic or desperate or visibly falling apart? Instead, I feel strangely clear, like my mind has simplified everything down to one idea and decided to sit there. Those calm scares me more than panic ever has. Panic feels like my body fighting for survival. This feels like my mind stepping back and quietly considering the option of not fighting anymore. There's no urgency in it, no countdown, no pressure to act. Just this steady awareness that letting go would mean not having to keep carrying all of this, and the fact that my brain can present that idea without alarm makes me feel like I don't fully know myself anymore.

I start watching my own thoughts more closely, not to fix them, but because I don't trust them the way I used to. I notice how easily they drift there when I'm tired, when I'm alone, when there's nothing demanding my attention. I notice how my body doesn't react with panic the way I expect it to. There's no spike of fear to pull me back, just this quiet acceptance that something inside me is very tired. That's when the fear creeps in. Not fear of dying, but fear of how normal this is starting to feel. Fear that my mind is adapting to something it shouldn't adapt to. Fear that if I stay here long enough, this calm will turn into indifference, and indifference feels like a place I might not be able to climb out of. I tell myself I'm still in control because I'm thinking about it, because I'm aware of it, because I haven't done anything. But that reassurance feels fragile. Awareness doesn't make the thoughts disappear. It just makes me more aware of how present they are, how quietly persistent they've become. I find myself wishing for panic, wishing for something loud enough to force action, something that would make it obvious to everyone, including me, that I need help.

This calm feels like being stuck in a fog where everything is muted and slowed, where even danger feels distant and abstract. And that's terrifying. Because it means I can sit with these thoughts for long stretches of time without reacting, without interrupting them, without feeling the kind of fear that usually keeps people safe. It means my mind can hold onto the idea of not existing and treat it like a hypothetical instead of a threat, and I don't know what that says about how far this has gone. I'm still here, I'm still functioning. But I don't feel anchored the way I used to. I feel like I'm floating just above my own life, detached enough that even something this serious can exist in my head without triggering the kind of response I expect. And that detachment makes everything feel unstable, like I'm standing on ground that looks solid but might give way at any moment. The calm doesn't comfort me. It alarms me. Because it tells me that this isn't just about fear anymore. This is about exhaustion reaching a level where even survival instincts start to quiet down, where rest starts to sound more appealing than resistance, and where the idea of stopping feels less like a threat and more like a possibility. I don't want that possibility. But I can feel how close it is, sitting there in the quiet, waiting for me to either push it away or let it stay. And right now, all I can do is notice it, feel the weight of it, and realize that I've reached a place where ignoring this isn't an option anymore, even if I don't yet know what acknowledging it will require of me.

Driving at night has always been my escape. The one place where I don't have to perform, don't have to explain myself, don't have to hold anything together for anyone else. Just the road, the darkness, the steady motion forward. It's where my thoughts usually settle, where the noise softens enough that I can breathe without feeling watched by my own mind. At least, that's how it used to be. Now, the car feels different. The silence isn't calming anymore. It's wide open. There's nothing to distract me, nothing to anchor me, nothing to pull my attention outward. The road stretches ahead of me, empty and endless, and instead of feeling free, I feel exposed. Alone with my thoughts in a way I didn't expect, in a place that was supposed to feel safe. The headlights cut through the dark, and everything else disappears. No houses. No people. Just movement and space. And in that space, the thoughts get louder. They don't rush in all at once. They settle in slowly, like they've been waiting for this moment. Waiting for me to stop talking, stop listening, stop filling the quiet with anything else. The drive becomes a container for everything I've been holding back, and once it opens, there's nowhere for it to go. I grip the steering wheel a little tighter without realizing it.

My body knows something is wrong before my mind wants to admit it. The sentence shows up again, steady and familiar. I can't live like this. It feels heavier out here, surrounded by nothing but darkness and motion. There's no room to soften it, no one to reassure, no version of myself I need to perform. Just me and the truth of how exhausted I feel. How tired I am of managing my own existence. How tempting it feels to imagine an end to the effort. I hate that this place has changed. This drive used to be where I processed things, where I let my thoughts move without overwhelming me. Now it feels like my mind is using the space against me, stretching the silence until the thoughts echo louder than they ever do during the day. The calm that scared me before feels even more dangerous here, wrapped in the steady hum of the engine and the rhythm of the road. I don't feel panicked. I don't feel out of control. And that's what terrifies me.

The thought of letting go doesn't come with fear here. It comes with this sense of release, like something inside me is finally allowed to rest. And the fact that my brain can sit with that idea so comfortably, so quietly, makes my chest tighten in a way panic never has. I tell myself this is just a drive. Just thoughts. Just a bad moment. But the road keeps going, and the thoughts stay with me, patient and persistent, filling the space where calm used to live. I realize, sitting there in the dark, that even my safest escape isn't safe anymore. There's nowhere left to run from my own mind. The drive doesn't soothe me this time. It exposes me. It forces me to sit with how far things have gone, with how tired I am, with how thin the line feels between wanting relief and wanting to disappear. And that realization lands hard, because it means I've lost one of the few places where I used to feel okay. I keep driving anyway. Because stopping doesn't feel safer, and going home doesn't feel safer either. All I know is that I'm alone with this now, in a place that was never supposed to hold this much weight, realizing that if even this escape has turned against me, then something is very wrong.

The road stops feeling like it's taking me anywhere. It turns into a loop, a stretch of darkness that keeps repeating itself no matter how long I drive. Mile after mile passes, but nothing shifts inside me. The movement that used to help me process now just keeps me suspended, like I'm circling the same thought without getting closer to an answer. I notice how automatic everything has become. My hands know where to go. My eyes stay fixed ahead. My body drives while my mind drifts, untethered, wandering places I don't want it to go.

There's no sense of destination anymore, just motion for the sake of motion, like I'm afraid of what might happen if I stop. The thoughts don't escalate. They deepen. They settle in with a kind of patience that feels unsettling, like they know I'm not running from them anymore. I'm just sharing space with them, letting them sit beside me in the quiet, feeling their weight without reacting. It feels less like a crisis and more like a resignation I don't fully understand yet. I realize how tired I am of trying to outrun this. Not just tonight, but in general. Tired of managing. Tired of coping. Tired of pretending I can outpace my own mind if I just keep moving. The drive turns into a metaphor I didn't ask for, me going forward without feeling like I'm actually going anywhere, repeating the same internal terrain over and over again. I start thinking about how long this has been building. How many days I've pushed through. How many times I've told myself tomorrow will be easier. How often I've chosen distraction over honesty because honesty felt too heavy to carry. And sitting here now, alone on the road, it all catches up to me at once. There's a moment where I realize I'm not searching for relief anymore. I'm searching for an exit from the effort itself. That thought lands differently than the others. It feels heavier. More final. Not in the sense that I'm planning anything, but in the sense that my mind has started categorizing existence itself as something that needs a way out. And that realization sends a quiet chill through me, because it tells me how far this has gone without me fully noticing. I don't feel dramatic, I don't feel overwhelmed, I feel worn down.

The road keeps stretching ahead of me, dark and empty, and I'm struck by how isolated this feels. Not just physically, but internally. There's no one here to interrupt my thoughts, no noise to break the rhythm, no reminder that I'm connected to anything outside this moment. Just me, the road, and the steady awareness that I can't keep living inside this loop. I slow down slightly without thinking about it. The act feels instinctive, like my body is responding to something my mind hasn't fully named yet. There's a heaviness in my chest, not sharp or urgent, just dense, like something pressing inward. I know, sitting here, that this drive isn't helping anymore. It isn't hurting me either, it's just revealing something. That the strategies I've relied on, the escapes I've trusted, aren't enough for what I'm carrying now. That the place I used to go to feel free has become another place where the truth catches up to me. And that realization feels like losing ground I didn't know I was standing on. The loop continues, the thoughts remain, and I'm left with the understanding that movement alone can't save me from this, that eventually I'm going to have to stop and face what's waiting when the engine goes quiet.

Being alone with my mind stops feeling like solitude and starts feeling like exposure. There's nowhere to redirect my attention now, no comforting illusion that this drive is helping me work through anything. The quiet isn't neutral anymore. It feels charged, like it's pressing in on me from all sides, asking me to acknowledge what I've been avoiding. I realize how long I've relied on noise to keep myself upright. Conversations. Music. Work. Distraction. Even movement. Anything that keeps my thoughts from settling too deeply. Sitting here, moving through the dark with nothing but the hum of the car and the road ahead, there's nothing left to buffer me from myself. The thoughts don't rush, they don't argue, they just exist. That's what makes them so heavy.

There's no spike of panic to warn me that something is wrong. No urgency pushing me to act. Just this steady presence, like my mind has decided this is a place it's comfortable returning to. And that comfort scares me in a way I can't explain without feeling ashamed of it. I start noticing how my body feels, how tense my shoulders are, how shallow my breathing has become without me meaning it to. It's like my body knows something my mind is still trying to minimize. Like it's holding me together while quietly signaling that I'm not okay. I think about how alone this feels. Not alone in the sense that no one cares, but alone in the sense that no one is here in this moment, inside this thought process, sitting with the exact weight I'm carrying right now. There's no one to interrupt it, no one to ground me just by their presence. Just me and the realization that I don't trust myself the way I used to. That thought lands hard. I've always trusted my own mind, even when it was anxious, even when it was overwhelmed. I trusted that it wanted to keep me alive, that it would push me toward safety when things got bad. Sitting here now, I'm not so sure. Not because I think it wants to hurt me, but because it seems tired of protecting me, tired of fighting, tired of carrying this much weight.

I tell myself I'm still in control. I tell myself I would never act on these thoughts. And both of those things feel true, but they don't bring the comfort I expect them to. Control doesn't feel solid when the thoughts are this persistent. Safety doesn't feel secure when relief keeps showing up in the same shape. I realize I'm scared of myself in a way I never have been before. Not scared that I'll do something, but scared of how convincing the quiet sounds, scared of how easy it is for my mind to drift toward the idea of stopping without triggering alarms. That fear doesn't explode. It settles. It sits with me, heavy and unmoving, making everything feel smaller and tighter. I'm still driving, still breathing, still here. The sense of being alone with this, truly alone in it, makes the night feel endless. It makes the road feel less like freedom and more like a corridor I'm trapped inside, moving forward because stopping feels just as frightening as continuing. I don't know how to fix this. I don't know how to talk myself out of it. All I know is that being alone with my mind like this feels like too much, and that realization shifts something inside me, because it tells me I'm reaching the edge of what I can manage by myself. And that thought doesn't bring relief. It brings a quiet, unmistakable fear that I've gone as far as I can go alone.

The sentence stops feeling like something I'm thinking and starts feeling like something I've arrived at. It doesn't come with urgency or emotion. It doesn't need emphasis. It just settles in, heavy and immovable, like a line drawn across the road that I can't drive past. I can't live like this. It's not a plea, It's not a threat, It's an assessment. I've thought versions of it before, softer ones, ones I could talk myself out of or dismiss as exaggeration. This one doesn't budge when I challenge it. It doesn't disappear when I distract myself. It doesn't change when I remind myself of reasons or responsibilities or future possibilities. It stays exactly where it is, solid and calm, like my body understands it before my mind tries to negotiate with it.

That's when I realize something important. This isn't about whether I want to live, it's about whether I can keep enduring life in this state. The distinction matters, even if it doesn't make things easier. I don't want to die. I don't feel pulled toward an act or a plan. What I feel is a hard stop inside me, like some internal system has finally reached its limit and shut something down. The constant pushing. The constant managing. The constant pretending. Something in me is done agreeing to that. I sit with that realization, letting it press against me, and notice how my body reacts. Not with panic, not with urgency, but with this deep, heavy stillness.

Like everything inside, me has gone quiet at the same time. It feels less like falling apart and more like hitting a wall I didn't know was there until I walked straight into it. I can't live like this. It repeats, not louder, just steadier, like it's anchoring itself deeper into me. I try to imagine continuing the way I have been, another week, another month, another year, and something inside me recoils so strongly that I must slow my breathing. The idea isn't just unpleasant. It feels impossible. And that's when I know I've reached something I can't undo. I can't go back to pretending I didn't know this. I can't convince myself this is just a rough patch that will resolve if I ignore it long enough. The sentence has crossed from thought to truth, from something I can debate to something I have to respond to, even if I don't know how yet.

I don't feel clarity. I don't feel courage. I feel cornered. Not by external circumstances, not by people or expectations, but by my own internal reality. By the fact that continuing the way I have been feels unbearable, and stopping feels terrifying, and there's no obvious path between those two truths yet. I stay on the road, letting the night pass around me, feeling the weight of that line settle into my chest. I don't know what comes next. I don't know what I'm supposed to do with this realization. All I know is that something fundamental has shifted, and there's no pretending my way out of it anymore. The bottom isn't a collapse, It's a limit. And I'm standing right up against it, aware for the first time that whatever happens next can't look like what came before.

The fear doesn't come from what I'm thinking. It comes from realizing how different this feels from anything I've known before. Anxiety has edges. Depression has weight. This has neither. This feels like my mind has reached a conclusion quietly, without drama, without protest, and that quiet certainty unsettles me more than chaos ever could. I start watching myself the way you watch something fragile, not because it's breaking loudly, but because it might break if handled the wrong way. I notice how carefully I'm thinking now, how deliberately I'm choosing which thoughts to engage with and which ones to let pass. I don't trust my mind the way I used to. I don't assume it's automatically on my side anymore. That realization lands heavy. It's strange to feel afraid of your own thoughts without feeling out of control. I'm still me. I still know who I am. I still know what I believe. And yet, there's this new awareness sitting underneath everything, telling me that my internal landscape has shifted into territory I don't recognize. That something serious is happening even though nothing looks dramatic on the outside. I think about how easily I could keep this to myself.

How simple it would be to drive home, go to bed, wake up, and keep functioning the way I always have. No one would know. No one would stop me. The thought that I could continue like these unnoticed feels terrifying in a way I can't fully explain. Not because I want intervention, but because it means I could disappear internally without anything forcing me to stop. That's when the fear turns inward. Not fear of acting. Fear of normalizing this. Fear that if I treat these thoughts like just another thing to manage, they'll sink deeper, settle more comfortably, become a background truth I carry everywhere. Fear that this quiet acceptance will slowly turn into something harder to climb out of, not because I chose it, but because I let it stay too long. I notice how alert I am now, how every thought feels important, how I'm scanning myself for signs that this is getting worse.

That vigilance doesn't calm me. It exhausts me. It makes everything feel precarious, like I'm standing on ground that could shift at any moment without warning. I don't feel like myself anymore. Not in a dramatic identity-shattering way, but in this subtle sense that something essential has changed. That the rules I've lived by don't fully apply here. That the tools I've relied on aren't enough for this level of quiet seriousness. And realizing that makes my chest tighten, because it means I'm facing something I can't simply think my way out of. I keep driving, but my attention isn't on the road anymore. It's turned inward completely, focused on this new awareness that's taken root. The understanding that this isn't just another bad night. This isn't just exhaustion. This is a line I've crossed internally, and I can't pretend I haven't. I don't feel dramatic, I don't feel desperate, I feel aware.

That awareness is heavy, because it comes with responsibility, I don't yet know how to carry. Responsibility to myself. To my life. To the fact that something is wrong in a way that requires more than endurance. The bottom isn't loud. It's clarifying. And sitting there in that clarity, alone with my thoughts, I realize that whatever comes next can't be handled the way I've handled everything else so far. Something about this moment demands a different response, even if I don't yet know what that response is.

The fear shifts again, quietly, without announcing itself. It's no longer just fear of the thoughts or fear of how calm they feel. It becomes fear of how alone I am with them. Fear of the fact that everything I've been doing up to this point—enduring, distracting, pretending—has reached its limit, and I'm standing here without a next move. I don't suddenly want to tell someone. I don't feel ready to explain anything. The idea of saying this out loud still feels overwhelming, like it would make everything too real, too irreversible. But something inside me recognizes that carrying this alone isn't working anymore, and that recognition lands heavy in my chest. I'm used to handling things by myself. I'm used to being the one who figures it out internally and then shows up like nothing happened. That identity has held me together for a long time. Sitting here now, it feels fragile. Not broken yet, but thin, stretched past what it was designed to hold. I realize how much effort it's taking just to keep myself steady in this moment. Not steady in a visible way, not in a way anyone else would notice, but steady enough not to spiral, not to drift further into thoughts I don't trust.

The energy it takes to maintain that balance is exhausting, and the idea of doing it indefinitely feels impossible. I don't know how to ask for help, I don't even know what help would look like. All I know is that I don't feel capable of navigating this by myself anymore, even though I've been doing exactly that for so long. That realization doesn't bring relief. It brings a new kind of weight, the weight of knowing I need something I don't yet know how to reach for. I think about how contained my life looks from the outside. How normal everything appears. How easy it would be for this to remain invisible. And instead of comforting me, that thought makes me feel hollow. It means there's nothing external forcing change. No alarm. No interruption.

Just me and the responsibility to take this seriously before it settles in deeper. I don't feel ready to act, I don't feel ready to speak. But I do feel something loosening inside me, like my grip on the idea that I can do this alone is weakening. Not collapsing, not shattering, just softening in a way that scares me because it means change is coming whether I initiate it or not. I slow the car again without thinking about it, like my body is trying to match the pace of my thoughts. The road is still dark. The night still quiet. Nothing around me has changed. And yet everything inside me feels different, like I'm standing at the edge of a realization that can't be undone. I don't know what the next step is, I don't know when it will happen. I just know that pretending my way through this is no longer an option, and that knowledge sits with me, heavy and unavoidable, as I keep moving forward into a future, I can't yet imagine navigating the way I've navigated everything else. Holding on doesn't feel heroic. It doesn't feel strong or brave or meaningful. It feels mechanical, like something my body is doing on instinct while my mind stays suspended somewhere between fear and numbness. I'm not gripping onto a reason. I'm not clinging to hope. I'm just… not letting go. There's a difference, and I can feel it. I'm not thinking about the future in any real way.

The idea of tomorrow doesn't comfort me, and it doesn't scare me either. It feels abstract, distant, like something that belongs to a different version of me. All I'm focused on is this moment, this stretch of time where I need to keep myself here without fully knowing why or how. It feels strange to admit that staying takes effort. Not effort in the way people talk about resilience, but effort in the way it takes effort to keep your eyes open when you're exhausted, effort to keep breathing when your chest feels heavy, effort to stay present when your mind keeps offering you ways to disappear from the weight of everything. I'm not choosing life with conviction.

I'm choosing it by default, because something in me refuses to take the other option, even when it sounds tempting. I don't feel proud of that. I feel scared of how thin the line feels between staying and not staying, how much of it seems to rest on momentum rather than intention. I keep moving because I'm already moving. I keep driving because I'm already on the road. I keep breathing because my body hasn't given me another choice. And that feels fragile. I notice how careful I am with myself now, how gently I'm thinking, how slowly I'm letting thoughts pass through without grabbing onto them. It's like I'm handling something breakable, aware that one wrong move could send me somewhere I don't want to go.

That awareness keeps me tethered, even as it exhausts me. I'm not fighting anymore. I'm not surrendering either. I'm hovering in this narrow space where all I can manage is staying present enough not to drift, grounded enough not to slip further into the quiet that scares me. It doesn't feel like living. It feels like maintenance. Like keeping a system running long enough to prevent a shutdown I don't know how to recover from. There's a strange clarity in that. I see how much pressure I've been under. How long I've been carrying things without setting them down. How my mind didn't break suddenly but slowly adapted to being overloaded until relief started sounding like an answer. That understanding doesn't fix anything, but it stops me from blaming myself in the way I usually do. This isn't weakness.

This is exhaustion. And acknowledging that feels important, even if it doesn't bring comfort. It tells me that something real is happening here, something that deserves attention instead of dismissal. It tells me that staying right now isn't about willpower, it's about recognizing my limits and not pushing past them blindly anymore. I don't know what I'm holding on to exactly. A sense of responsibility, maybe. A quiet instinct. A refusal to let this moment define the end of my story. I just know that letting go feels final in a way I'm not ready for, and that's enough to keep me here for now. The road continues. The night stays quiet. And I stay too, not because I feel strong, but because something in me hasn't given up yet, even if it doesn't know what it's holding out for.

The panic doesn't announce itself the way I expect it to. There's no rush of adrenaline, no racing heart, no frantic urge to escape. It settles in quietly, heavy and dense, like the air itself has thickened and I'm breathing through something I can't see. It feels internal, contained, almost polite in how it takes up space. That's how I know how low this is. I've always associated panic with chaos, with losing control in a way that's obvious and disruptive. This isn't that. This is the kind of panic that comes from understanding something you can't un-know. From realizing you've reached a place you never thought you'd reach and there's no dramatic moment to mark it, just a steady awareness that this is the lowest you've ever been.

I don't feel like I'm falling, I feel like I've already landed. There's a weight in my chest that doesn't lift when I shift positions or take deeper breaths. It isn't sharp. It isn't urgent. It just sits there, constant, like my body is holding onto something my mind hasn't fully processed yet. I feel slowed down, like everything inside me is moving through thick resistance. I think about how normal I must look if anyone could see me right now. Just driving. Just existing. Nothing about this moment looks dangerous or alarming from the outside. And that thought makes the panic heavier, because it means this bottom is invisible.

There's no signal going out. No interruption coming. Just me, sitting inside an internal collapse no one else can see. I start to understand how people can reach places like this quietly. Not because they're dramatic or reckless, but because they're tired. Because they've been holding things together for so long that when the system finally reaches its limit, it doesn't explode. It shuts down piece by piece. And sitting here now, I can feel how close I am to that edge, how easy it would be to disappear internally without anyone noticing the moment it happened. That awareness presses in on me. This is the lowest place I've ever been, not because of how bad it feels, but because of how settled it feels. Because of how little resistance my mind offers to the idea that I can't keep going like this. Because of how close relief feels without feeling dramatic or desperate. I don't feel hysterical, I feel cornered. Cornered by my own limits. Cornered by the fact that endurance has run out and there's nothing left to replace it yet. Cornered by the knowledge that something must change, even though I don't know how to make that change happen.

The panic isn't loud enough to force action. It's just loud enough to keep me awake to the reality of where I am. It's the kind that sits with you, breathing alongside you, making sure you understand that this isn't something you can minimize or push through the way you always have. I stay on the road, feeling the weight of that understanding settle deeper into me. This isn't a moment I'll forget. This isn't something I can talk myself out of later. This is a floor, solid and undeniable, and I'm standing on it whether I'm ready to acknowledge it or not. I've hit bottom. Not in a way that looks dramatic, not in a way anyone else can see, but in a way that changes how I understand myself, how I understand my limits, and how seriously I need to take what's happening inside me. Once I name it as bottom, everything goes quiet in a different way. Not the dangerous calm from before, not the seductive stillness that made letting go sound easy, but a heavier kind of stillness that comes from knowing I've reached a limit I can't negotiate past. It feels like my mind has stopped arguing with itself and is just sitting there, letting the truth exist without trying to soften it. This happened. I can't undo it. I can't un-know it. I can't convince myself it was just a bad night or a temporary dip.

Something fundamental has been exposed, and pretending otherwise would mean lying to myself in a way I'm no longer capable of doing. That realization doesn't bring clarity. It brings gravity. I notice how careful I am now, like I'm walking through my own thoughts on uneven ground. I'm not pushing. I'm not forcing. I'm watching. Listening. Letting each thought pass through without grabbing onto it, because grabbing feels risky. Everything feels delicate, like I've cracked something open and don't yet know how to protect it. There's a strange stillness that comes with that awareness. Not peace. Not relief. Just a pause where nothing feels negotiable anymore. I don't feel dramatic about it. I don't feel like I need to mark the moment or assign it meaning. I just feel changed in a quiet, internal way, like I've crossed into a different understanding of myself. I know now how far my mind can go when it's exhausted. I know what relief can sound like when it's wearing the wrong disguise. And that knowledge settles into me slowly, like something I'll be carrying for a long time. I start thinking about how easy it would be to pretend this never happened once I get home. To go back to functioning. To put the mask back on and keep everything moving. The thought crosses my mind automatically, and then it stops, because I know I can't do that anymore. Not fully. I might still function. I might still show up. I might still smile and talk and move through my days. But something inside me won't let me believe the lie that this is just something I can power through on my own. The floor I'm standing on is too solid.

The weight of it is too real. I don't know what comes next. I don't know what acknowledging this will require of me. All I know is that this moment exists now, undeniable and heavy, and it deserves to be taken seriously. Not with panic. Not with urgency. But with honesty. I keep driving, not to escape, not to process, just to exist inside this awareness for a little longer. The night stays dark. The road stays quiet. Nothing external shifts to mark what's happened inside me. But I know. And that knowing, even without answers, even without a plan, even without hope yet, feels like a turning point I can't step back from. Not because it fixes anything, but because it removes the option of pretending this wasn't real. I've hit bottom, and I'm still here, not healed, not steady, but aware enough now that something has to change, even if I don't yet know how.

The drive doesn't end with relief. It ends because it must. The road eventually loops back into familiarity, into streets I recognize, into a life that hasn't changed even though I have. The engine hums the same way it always does. The night looks the same. Nothing external marks what just happened. I pull back into the world like nothing is wrong. That's the part that feels heaviest. Carrying this knowledge forward into a life that still expects me to function, to participate, to be okay enough. There's no dramatic transition between bottom and normalcy. There's just the shift from being alone with the truth to having to hold it quietly inside me again. I feel different stepping out of the car. Not fragile exactly but altered. Like something has been exposed that can't be covered up the same way anymore. I move carefully, not because I'm afraid of falling apart, but because I'm aware of how close I came to a place I never wanted to reach. The sentence stays with me. I can't live like this. It doesn't fade with movement. It doesn't soften when I change environments. It settles into me, not as a threat, but as a boundary. A line my body and mind have drawn together, saying this is as far as you can go pretending nothing is wrong. I don't feel urgency yet; I don't feel hope. I feel responsibility. Responsibility to myself, in a way I haven't felt before. Not the pressure-filled kind that tells me to do better or be stronger, but the quiet kind that says this matters and you can't ignore it.

The weight of that responsibility is sobering. It makes everything feel slower, more deliberate, like I'm walking through my life with an added gravity I didn't have before. I notice how tired I am, not just physically, but in my bones, in my thoughts, in the way even standing still feels like effort. This isn't a tired that can be slept off. This is the kind that comes from reaching a limit and realizing how long I've been pushing past it without noticing. I don't feel fixed by this realization. I don't feel saved by it. But I do feel changed. There's a quiet seriousness that settles in, replacing the numb calm from before. A sense that something important has happened, even if I don't yet know how to respond to it. I'm no longer just surviving on autopilot. I'm aware of the cost of doing that, and that awareness makes it impossible to go back to ignorance. I move through the rest of the night carrying that weight, careful not to jostle it, not to push it away, not to pretend it isn't there. I don't tell myself things will get better. I don't promise myself anything. I just acknowledge that this moment now exists in my story, whether I want it to or not. The bottom didn't end me, but it marked me. And as the night gives way to the idea of morning, I understand that even though nothing looks different yet, something fundamental has shifted.

The way I've been living has reached its end, not with a bang, not with collapse, but with a quiet, unmistakable knowing that I can't keep going the same way. Whatever comes next isn't here yet. But this moment is. The bottom isn't dramatic when I finally stand on it. There's no collapse, no moment where everything shatters at once. It's solid. Unmoving. A floor that doesn't give way beneath me, even though part of me expected it to. I don't fall through it. I don't disappear into it. I just… stop. I stop pushing. I stop pretending this is manageable. I stop believing I can outlast this on my own. That's what bottom really is for me. Not an ending, not a decision, but the moment my body and mind agree that something has reached its limit. The moment where survival stops looking like endurance and starts looking like simply staying put, breathing, not letting go even when letting go sounds peaceful. I'm still here.

That fact surprises me more than anything else. After everything my mind has offered me, after how tempting relief has sounded, after how close I've come to wanting everything to stop, I'm still here. Not because I feel hopeful. Not because I feel strong. Just because something in me refuses to disappear quietly. That refusal isn't loud, It isn't confident. It's instinctual. I don't make promises to myself. I don't swear things will get better. I don't suddenly see a future worth fighting for. All I know is that tonight didn't end me, even though it scared me in a way nothing else ever has. And that matters, even if I don't know what to do with that knowledge yet. The bottom feels cold and real beneath my feet. There's no illusion left here. No story I can tell myself to soften it. I know now how far my mind can go when it's exhausted. I know what relief can masquerade as. I know that pretending nearly cost me more than I was willing to lose. And knowing that changes something. Not everything. Not yet. But something important. I don't climb out of the bottom in this moment. I don't rise. I don't transform. I just stay. I let the truth sit where it belongs.

I let myself exist without asking for more, without demanding answers, without forcing meaning out of pain that hasn't settled yet. This is the lowest point I've ever reached. And I'm still breathing inside it. That doesn't feel like victory. It feels like reality. And right now, reality is enough to keep me here, enough to keep the night from swallowing me whole, enough to remind me that even when my mind is begging for rest, disappearing isn't the only way to get it. The bottom doesn't save me, but it doesn't take me either. It just holds me, long enough for the next part of my life to become possible, even if I can't see it yet. And that's where this chapter ends. Not with hope, not with answers, just with the truth that I hit bottom, and I didn't vanish.

Chapter 9

Asking for Help – Therapy, doctors, and fear

Exhaustion doesn't feel like collapse. It feels like a dull settling, like everything inside me has slowed down without stopping entirely. I'm still thinking. Still aware. Still moving through my days. But the energy it takes to keep negotiating with myself is gone, and what's left is this quiet, heavy stillness that doesn't ask questions anymore. I know I need help. That thought exists without urgency, without drama, without resistance. It's just there, fully formed, undeniable. I don't argue with it the way I used to. I don't try to rationalize it away. I don't convince myself I can handle this alone forever. The knowing has settled in deep enough that it doesn't need defending. And still, I don't reach out. Not because I don't believe in help. Not because I think I'm above it. But because the idea of opening that door feels heavier than carrying what I already have. Asking for help feels like adding something new to an already overloaded system, like introducing another variable I don't have the capacity to manage. I sit with the awareness quietly, letting it exist without turning it into action. There's no panic attached to it now. Just fatigue. The kind that makes even necessary steps feel impossible, not because they're wrong, but because they require energy I don't have. I think about what help would mean. Not in practical terms. Not appointments or names or processes.

I think about what it would cost me internally. The privacy I'd lose. The control I'd give up. The way my internal world would stop being just mine once I let someone else see it. And that cost feels too high right now, even knowing what staying silent is costing me too. I don't feel torn anymore. I feel paused. Like I'm standing in place, aware of every option in front of me, but unable to move toward any of them. The exhaustion has flattened everything into the same level of difficulty. Reaching out feels just as overwhelming as continuing alone, and so I do neither. I just stay where I am, suspended between knowing and doing. There's a strange clarity in that stillness. I'm not confused about what I need. I'm not in denial about how serious this is. I'm simply too tired to take the next step, too depleted to initiate change, even when I know it's necessary. That truth sits with me quietly, without judgment, without urgency, just waiting. I don't tell myself I'll ask for help tomorrow, I don't promise myself anything. I let the thought exist without resolution, without timeline, without expectation. It's there, steady and heavy, like a door I can see clearly now but don't yet have the strength to touch. And so I remain here, not choosing silence out of stubbornness or pride, but out of sheer exhaustion. Aware. Resistant. Still. Not reaching out. Not falling apart. Just suspended in the space between knowing I need help and not being able to ask for it yet.

Knowing that help exists doesn't comfort me the way people say it should. It doesn't feel reassuring or grounding. It feels heavier, like a responsibility I didn't ask for has been placed directly in my hands. Once you know there are options, pretending you're unaware stops working, and the weight of not acting becomes its own kind of pressure. I'm aware of therapists,

aware of doctors, aware of resources and paths and next steps. That awareness sits with me constantly, not urging me forward, just existing there, like a quiet reminder I can't turn off. It follows me through my days, through moments that look normal from the outside, through routines that haven't changed even though my internal world has. Knowing help is there doesn't move me toward it.

It makes staying where I am feeling more deliberate, more charged. I catch myself thinking about what it would mean to reach out, not in terms of improvement, but in terms of consequence. What would shift the moment I say it out loud. What would no longer belong only to me. The privacy I'd lose feels tangible, like something I can already feel slipping away just by considering it. There's a strange pressure that comes with knowing help exists, because it removes the excuse of ignorance. I can't tell myself I don't know what to do anymore. I know exactly what I could do. I just don't feel capable of doing it, and that gap between knowledge and action feels uncomfortable in a way that's hard to sit with.

I don't feel guilty for not reaching out, I feel stuck. Stuck in this place where awareness doesn't translate into movement, where knowing doesn't turn into doing, where understanding my situation doesn't bring clarity about how to change it. The options don't feel like lifelines. They feel like doors that require more energy than I have to open. I notice how often my mind drifts toward the idea of help and then gently turns away from it, not dramatically, not forcefully, just with a quiet no that feels final in the moment. It's not rejection. It's preservation. The sense that introducing something new right now would overwhelm me more than it would help. So, I keep carrying this knowledge without acting on it, letting it sit beside everything else I'm already holding. It doesn't make things better. It doesn't make them worse. It just adds another layer to the suspension I'm living in, another truth I'm aware of but not ready to respond to. Help exists; I know that. And knowing it doesn't pull me forward yet.

It just deepens the stillness, making the space I'm stuck in feel more defined, more intentional, like I'm choosing not to move even though I understand exactly what movement would look like. I stay there, in that awareness, letting the thought of help remain what it is for now: something real, something necessary, and something I'm not ready to reach for, even as it waits quietly within reach.

Privacy starts to feel like the last thing I still control. Not in a dramatic way, not like I'm guarding a secret out of pride, but in the way you hold onto something small when everything else feels like it's slipping through your hands. Keeping this to myself feels like the only boundary I haven't crossed yet, the only line that hasn't been blurred. Once someone else knows, it won't be long just to me anymore. I think about how quickly things change once words leave your mouth. How something internal becomes external the moment it's named. How explanations begin, questions follow, concern settles in. I imagine my thoughts being translated into someone else's language, turned into notes or labels or plans, and the idea makes my chest tighten. Not because I don't want understanding, but because I don't trust what understanding might cost me.

Silence feels safer. Not because it's healthy, not because it's right, because it's familiar. I've learned how to live inside this. I know how to manage my days, how to keep my face steady, how to keep my voice even, how to move through the world without drawing attention to the weight I'm carrying. Speaking would disrupt that balance. It would invite interpretation. It would open a door I can't close once it's open. I don't want to be watched. I don't want concern hovering over me, waiting for signs, measuring my moods, interpreting my quiet moments. I don't want to become something fragile in other people's eyes, even if I already feel fragile inside. The idea of being seen differently feels heavier than the idea of continuing quietly the way I am.

Privacy isn't about hiding; it's about staying intact. I tell myself that if I keep this contained, I can still decide how it unfolds. That as long as it stays inside me, I'm the one in charge of how much space it takes up, when it surfaces, when it stays quiet. Letting someone else in feels like handing that control over, and I'm not ready to do that. So, I choose silence deliberately. Not out of denial. Not out of ignorance. Out of fear that once this is shared, it won't be mine anymore, and I don't know who I'll be once that happens. I don't know how to exist in a version of my life where my inner world is open for discussion, assessment, or intervention. For now, keeping it private feels like the only way I can breathe without feeling exposed. The only way I can exist without being defined by something I'm still trying to understand myself. And even though I know that silence comes with its own cost, it's the cost I recognize, the cost I know how to pay. I stay quiet, holding onto privacy like it's a lifeline, even as I sense how thin it's becoming. Even as I know that this control is temporary. Even as I understand that eventually, something will have to give.

But not yet. Not now.

I remain suspended here, choosing silence not because I believe it will save me, but because right now, it's the only thing that feels like it's still mine. Therapy doesn't feel like help when I think about it. It feels like exposure. Like sitting in a room where everything I've kept contained finally has a place to spill, whether I'm ready for it or not. I don't picture relief or understanding. I picture myself being seen in a way I can't control. The idea of talking isn't what scares me. It's what talking turns into. Once the words exist outside of me, they stop being flexible.

They stop being something I can soften or reframe or minimize in my own head. They become something that can be repeated back to me, something that can be interpreted, something that can be written down and remembered in ways I might not be ready for. I don't want to hear myself say it out loud. I don't want to hear my thoughts arranged into sentences that sound more serious than they feel inside me. I don't want to watch someone else's face change as I speak, don't want to wonder which words crossed a line, don't want to feel the moment where concern shifts into assessment. That moment feels terrifying to imagine, like a point of no return.

Therapy feels like being translated. Like my internal world would be turned into language that doesn't quite fit me anymore. Reduced to explanations and categories that flatten something deeply personal into something clinical. I'm afraid that once it's framed that way, I'll lose the ability to understand myself on my own terms.

I don't want to be reduced to symptoms. I don't want to sit there and wonder which version of myself is being seen, or whether the person across from me is seeing all of me or just the parts that sound the most alarming. I don't trust myself to explain it well enough, and I don't trust the process not to miss the nuance that feels so important to me. There's also the fear of finality.

Once I say it out loud, I can't pretend it was just a phase or a bad stretch or something I exaggerated in my head. Speaking makes it real in a way that thinking doesn't. And I'm not sure I'm ready for that level of reality yet, even if part of me knows I'm already living inside it. So when I think about therapy, I don't feel supported. I feel cornered. Like the act of asking for help would require me to give up the last bit of control I still have over how this exists in my life. And that feels like too much to surrender when I already feel stretched thin. I tell myself I'm not avoiding it forever. Just not now. I stay in that reasoning, letting it hold me in place.

Therapy remains something distant, something theoretical, something I acknowledge without moving toward. Not because I don't believe it could help, but because the cost of being fully seen feels heavier than the cost of continuing to carry this alone. For now, exposure feels more dangerous than silence. And so I stay where I am, suspended between knowing I need support and fearing what that support would require me to reveal. Doctors feel different. Less emotional, more final. When I think about seeing a doctor, my mind doesn't go to conversation or understanding, it goes straight to outcomes. To decisions being made quickly. To words like treatment and medication and plan. To something being prescribed that I'm expected to take every day, indefinitely, without knowing who I'll be once it becomes part of my routine. The idea of medication scares me more than I want to admit. Not because I think it's wrong. Not because I judge anyone who needs it. But because relying on something every day feels like admitting this isn't temporary, like agreeing that this is now part of my identity whether I want it to be or not. I don't want to wake up each morning knowing I need something just to be okay enough to function. I don't want my stability to feel conditional.

There's fear in the permanence of it. Once you start, it feels like you can't easily stop. Like you've crossed into a version of life that requires maintenance forever. I worry about what it would change, what it would dull, what it would sharpen. I worry about losing parts of myself I still recognize, parts I'm clinging to as proof that I'm still me underneath all of this. Seeing a doctor feels like handing my body and mind over to a system that doesn't know me the way I know myself. I imagine sitting there, trying to compress everything I've been living with into a short explanation, knowing it will never fully capture the nuance of how these feels. I imagine decisions being made based on fragments, based on checklists and symptoms and timelines that don't reflect the complexity of my inner world. And that makes me want to pull back before I even step forward. I don't want to be managed. I don't want my days to revolve around dosages, side effects, adjustments.

I don't want to wonder if a good day is really mine or if it belongs to something I swallowed that morning. The loss of autonomy feels real in those thoughts, heavy enough to keep me frozen where I am. So I tell myself I'll manage without it. I convince myself that as long as I'm still functioning, still showing up, still getting through the day, I don't need to introduce something so permanent into my life. I hold onto the idea that needing medication would mean I've crossed a line I'm not ready to acknowledge yet. And beneath all of that is a quieter fear. If I see a doctor, I won't just be explaining how I feel. I'll be asking them to decide how serious this is. And I don't know if I'm ready to hear that answer. I don't know if I'm ready to sit with someone else's judgment about something I've been trying so hard to contain on my own. So doctors stay distant in my mind. A possibility I'm aware of but actively avoid. Another door I can see clearly and still refuse to open, not because I don't believe in what's on the other side, but because I'm afraid of what it would mean to step through it.

The deeper fear under all of it is losing autonomy. Not in an abstract way, not philosophically, but in a very real, physical sense. The idea that once I ask for help, I won't be the one steering anymore. That decisions will start happening around me, about me, without me fully understanding when or how I lost my say. I've spent so long holding myself together through control. Control over what I show. Control over what I say. Control over how much space this takes up in my life. Even when everything inside me feels unstable, that control gives me something solid to stand on. The thought of handing it over, even partially, makes my chest tighten. I worry about what happens once the truth is out there. I worry that concern will turn into monitoring. That help will turn into supervision. That honesty will turn into restrictions I didn't ask for. I imagine being told what I should do, how I should feel, what steps I need to take next, and the idea makes me want to retreat back into myself even further. I don't want to be managed. I don't want to be contained. I don't want my life to shrink because someone decides it needs to be safer.

There's a part of me that believes if I ask for help, I won't be trusted with myself anymore. That I'll lose the quiet freedom I still have, even if that freedom comes with suffering. I'm afraid of being protected in a way that feels suffocating, of being helped in a way that takes choice away instead of giving it back. That fear doesn't come from logic. It comes from instinct. An instinct to hold on to what little control I have left, even when it's heavy, even when it hurts. Control feels like dignity. It feels like ownership over my own experience. Letting go of it feels like admitting I can't be trusted with my own mind, and I'm not ready to accept that. So I stay where I am. Not because it's comfortable. Not because it's sustainable. But because it's familiar, and familiarity feels safer than uncertainty right now.

I tell myself that as long as I'm still here, still functioning, still choosing to stay, I haven't lost control. I cling to that idea, even as I sense how fragile it is. Asking for help feels like stepping into a system that has its own rules, its own thresholds, its own definitions of safety and risk. And I'm terrified that once I'm inside it, I won't know how to get back out. That I'll have crossed a line that can't be uncrossed. So, I hold the door shut from my side. I stay suspended in this place where autonomy still feels intact, even if it's costing me more than I want to admit. I tell myself that as long as I'm choosing silence, I'm choosing myself. Even if that choice is slowly exhausting me, even if it's built on fear, it's still mine. For now.

Hospitalization sits in my mind like a shadow I don't like to look at directly. I don't talk about it. I don't name it out loud. But it's there, hovering behind every thought of asking for help, shaping my hesitation in ways I don't always consciously recognize. The fear isn't dramatic. It's quiet and specific. I imagine saying the wrong thing. I imagine being too honest. I imagine a moment where concern shifts into action before I can catch it, where my words are no longer just words but evidence. Evidence that something needs to be done *to* me, not *with* me. And that thought makes my stomach drop. I don't want to be taken somewhere I didn't choose.

The idea of being removed from my life, even temporarily, feels suffocating. Being told where to go, when to sleep, what to do. Having my autonomy replaced by protocols and precautions. I picture myself trying to explain that I'm still here, still thinking, still capable, and feeling like none of it matters once the system decides I'm a risk. That loss of voice terrifies me. It's not that I don't understand why those systems exist. I do. I know they're meant to protect. But protection can feel a lot like confinement when you're the one inside it. And I don't trust myself to navigate that experience without losing something essential, something I might not get back once it's taken. I worry that one honest sentence could change everything. That there's a line I don't fully see, and once I cross it, I won't be able to step back. I won't be able to say wait, I didn't mean it like that, I'm not that bad, I just needed to say it out loud. The finality of that possibility keeps me silent, careful, measured in ways that feel exhausting. I don't want my worst thoughts to define me. I don't want a moment of exhaustion to be treated like a permanent state. I don't want my fear to be mistaken for danger. And yet, I don't trust that those distinctions would be understood once I'm inside a system that must prioritize safety over nuance.

So, the fear lingers. It sits between me and every potential step toward help, whispering about locked doors and loss of control and being trapped in a version of myself I don't recognize. It tells me that once I ask for help, I might not get to decide what help looks like anymore. And that thought keeps me exactly where I am. Still aware. Still exhausted. Still choosing silence, not because I don't need support, but because the risk of being misunderstood feels heavier than the pain of carrying this alone.

The fear tightens into something more personal when I imagine being seen as a threat. Not just to myself, but as someone who needs to be contained, monitored, protected from their own mind. That idea feels heavier than any diagnosis, heavier than any label. It feels like a misunderstanding I wouldn't know how to correct once it takes shape. I don't see myself that way. I don't feel dangerous. I feel tired. I feel worn down. I feel like I've reached a place where continuing alone isn't working, but that doesn't mean I've lost my sense of right and wrong, or my ability to choose, or my desire to stay. The fear is that nuance won't survive the moment I say too much. I imagine someone hearing only the worst part of what I've lived with and missing everything else. Missing the restraint. The awareness. The effort it takes to stay grounded. Missing the fact that even at my lowest, I'm still choosing to be here, still holding myself back from crossing lines I don't want to cross.

That fear makes me quiet. It makes me careful with my thoughts, careful even with myself, like I'm constantly editing my internal experience so it doesn't sound worse than it is. I hate that I do that. I hate that fear of being misunderstood shapes how honest I'm willing to be, even in my own head. Being seen as a threat feels like losing my humanity. Like being reduced to a risk instead of a person. Like my exhaustion would be interpreted as instability, my honesty as danger. I don't want to be watched for signs. I don't want my silence to be seen as suspicious. I don't want to exist under a lens that assumes I can't be trusted with my own life.

So, I keep things contained. I tell myself that as long as I stay quiet, I stay in control of how I'm perceived. As long as no one knows the full truth, I can still move through the world without being treated differently, without feeling like my every action is being evaluated for risk. That fear doesn't come from paranoia, it comes from vulnerability. From knowing how fragile context can be once you hand it over to someone else. From knowing how easily a story can change once it's no longer just yours to tell. And the idea of losing that control, of being seen through a filter I didn't choose, feels unbearable.

So, I stay silent, even when it costs me. Even when carrying this alone is exhausting. Even when I know that silence isn't sustainable forever. Because being misunderstood feels more dangerous than being alone right now. And that fear settles in beside everything else I'm carrying, another weight added to the suspension I'm living in, another reason the door to help stays closed, even as I stand right in front of it.

The fear of being looked at differently settles in quietly, like a grief I didn't expect to feel yet. It isn't about rejection. It's about change. About the way people's eyes soften when they're worried.

About conversations slowing down. About pauses where there used to be ease. I imagine that shift happening the moment the truth leaves my mouth, and it feels like something precious slipping away. I think about how I'm seen now. As capable. Reliable. Normal enough. I think about how much of my identity lives in that perception, how much safety there is in being unremarkable, in blending into the rhythm of everyday life without anyone watching too closely. The idea of losing that feels heavier than I want to admit. Once people know, they can't un-know. I imagine being treated gently in ways that feel wrong, like I'm suddenly breakable when I don't feel that way inside. I imagine concern replacing trust, questions replacing assumptions, my silence being read as something it never used to be. Even kindness starts to feel threatening when it carries the weight of worry behind it. I don't want to be pitied.

I don't want my struggles to become the first thing people see when they look at me. I don't want to feel like I have to reassure others about my own stability, like I need to manage their fear on top of my own. The thought of carrying that responsibility makes me want to retreat even further. There's grief in that imagined future. Grief for the ease of being taken at face value. Grief for the version of myself who could move through the world without explanation, without context, without concern trailing behind them. I miss that version already, even though I haven't said anything yet, even though nothing has changed on the surface. I realize how much I value being seen as whole. Not perfect. Not untouched by struggle. Just whole enough not to be handled differently. The fear is that once I speak, that wholeness will fracture in other people's eyes, and I'll be left trying to piece it back together while also navigating my own internal mess. So I stay quiet, protecting not just my privacy, but the way I exist in other people's lives. I tell myself I'm sparing them worry. I tell myself

I'm preserving normalcy. And part of me believes that, even as another part knows I'm also protecting myself from the pain of being seen in a new, unfamiliar way. That imagined shift lingers with me.

It makes the idea of asking for help feel like a loss as much as a step forward. A trade I'm not sure I'm ready to make. I'm not afraid of being judged. I'm afraid of being changed in someone else's mind before I've even figured out how to change inside my own. So, I remain here, holding onto the version of myself that still feels intact to the outside world, even as the inside grows heavier. Even as the cost of silence continues to add up.

Even as I know that this protection can't last forever. For now, I let the grief sit quietly beside me, another reason I don't reach out, another layer of suspension holding me in place. Silence stops feeling like something that's happening to me and starts feeling like something I'm choosing. Not impulsively. Not out of denial. Deliberately. I recognize the decision forming and, for once, I don't fight it. I accept it for what it is: an act of self-protection, even if it isn't a healthy one. I'm not pretending this is fine. I'm not convincing myself I don't need support. I'm choosing not to ask.

That distinction matters to me. It gives me back a sense of agency in a situation where so much feels out of my control. Staying quiet becomes a way to slow things down, to keep the world from reacting before I'm ready to deal with the consequences of that reaction. It feels like holding the brakes instead of accelerating into something I can't reverse. I tell myself I'm buying time. Time to understand what I'm feeling. Time to see if this shifts on its own. Time to gather strength I don't currently have. Silence becomes a pause button, even if I know it isn't a solution. There's a strange comfort in not moving, in letting things stay exactly as they are for a little longer. Movement feels risky. Stillness feels controlled. I'm aware of the cost, though. I feel it in the way everything feels heavier than it should. In the effort it takes to keep my thoughts from spiraling. In the way exhaustion lingers no matter how much I rest. I know I'm paying for this choice daily, quietly, without relief. But paying a known cost feels safer than stepping into an unknown one. I don't frame this as avoidance in my own mind.

I frame it as survival. As doing what I need to do to get through each day without adding another layer of fear or uncertainty. I remind myself that asking for help doesn't disappear as an option just because I'm not choosing it right now. That belief keeps me steady. I hold onto the idea that silence is temporary, even if I don't know when it will end. I don't promise myself I'll speak up tomorrow or next week. I just allow myself to stay where I am without turning that into failure or shame.

There's a quiet resolve in that. Not strength. Not confidence. Just a decision to remain intact for as long as I can. To protect myself in the only way that feels possible right now. I know this choice won't last forever. I can feel that. But today, it's the one that lets me keep breathing without feeling overwhelmed by what comes next. So, I stay silent on purpose, fully aware of what I'm doing and why. I hold the door shut from the inside, not because I don't know what's on the other side, but because I need a little more time before I'm ready to face it. And that choice, for now, is enough to keep me here.

Self-reliance has always been something I've been proud of. The ability to carry things quietly. To handle my own weight without asking anyone else to hold it for me. For a long time, that felt like strength, like proof that I was capable and grounded and dependable. Sitting here now, I start to see how thin that line really is. What once felt empowering now feels isolating. The more I rely on myself to manage this, the smaller my world becomes. Not in obvious ways, not socially or externally, but internally. My thoughts circle the same few places. My coping strategies narrow. My perspective tightens. I don't feel supported by my independence anymore. I feel enclosed by it. I realize how rarely I let anyone see uncertainty in me. How practiced I am at smoothing things over, at presenting a version of myself that doesn't invite questions. That habit used to feel protective. Now it feels like a wall I built so carefully that I don't know how to step around it without tearing something down. I tell myself I'm strong for handling this alone. I tell myself others don't need to worry. But there's a cost to that story, and I feel it every day. I feel it in the quiet moments when there's no one to check in with, no one who knows how much effort it takes just to stay steady. I feel it in the way I monitor myself constantly, like I'm both the patient and the caretaker, never getting a break from either role. There's no relief in that, only responsibility. The isolation isn't dramatic.

It's subtle. It shows up as emotional distance, as a lack of shared language for what I'm experiencing, as the sense that even when I'm surrounded by people, I'm carrying something alone that no one else can see or touch. That kind of isolation doesn't scream. It hums quietly in the background, steady and persistent. I start to notice how much pressure I've put on myself to be okay. Not happy. Not thriving. Just okay enough not to disrupt anything. That pressure used to motivate me. Now it exhausts me. It keeps me in this narrow space were asking for help feels like failure, and continuing alone feels like obligation. I don't feel heroic for managing this by myself anymore. I feel tired of being the only one who knows.

That realization shifts something inside me. Not enough to push me toward action yet, but enough to crack the belief that doing this alone is somehow better. Enough to see that what I've been calling strength might also be the thing keeping me stuck. I'm still choosing silence. I'm still not reaching out. But the story I tell myself about that choice is starting to change. It's no longer about pride or capability. It's about fear and fatigue and not knowing how to let anyone else into a space I've been guarding for so long. Self-reliance hasn't saved me. It's kept me contained. And sitting with that truth, even without acting on it, makes the space around me feel tighter, like I'm finally seeing the shape of the cage I've been standing inside without realizing it had walls.

The stalemate settles in quietly, like two truths standing across from each other with nowhere to go. I know I need help. That isn't up for debate anymore. It doesn't scare me to admit it, not internally. What scares me is that knowing doesn't come with movement. It just exists, heavy and unresolved, pressing against everything else I'm carrying. I need help. I can't ask for it. Both of those statements feel equally true, and neither one cancels the other out. I don't try to argue my way out of it anymore.

I don't look for loopholes or timelines or promises to myself about when I'll be ready. I just sit inside the tension of it, aware of how uncomfortable it is and how little room there is to maneuver. It feels like being stuck in a doorway, not fully inside, not fully outside. I replay the same internal conversations over and over, each one ending in the same place. If I reach out, I lose control. If I don't, I keep carrying this alone. Both options feel unbearable in different ways, and so I choose neither. I stay suspended, letting time pass without resolution, hoping that something will shift on its own.

The exhaustion makes everything feel slower. Even thinking about asking takes energy I don't have. The idea of explaining myself, of answering questions, of sitting with someone else's reaction feels overwhelming. At the same time, continuing like this feels just as heavy. There's no clear relief in either direction, just different kinds of weight. I notice how carefully I'm living now. How much attention I give to my own thoughts. How deliberately I avoid certain spirals. How much effort goes into maintaining this balance, into keeping myself from tipping too far in either direction. It's exhausting in a way that doesn't look like exhaustion from the outside. It looks like functioning. It looks like normalcy. It looks like nothing is wrong. Inside, it feels like holding two opposing truths without letting either one win. I don't feel dramatic about it. I don't feel hopeless. I feel stuck in a place that doesn't move unless I move it, and I don't yet know how to do that. The stalemate becomes its own reality, something I live inside of every day, something I carry with me quietly as I go through motions that haven't changed. I don't hate myself for this.

That's something new. I don't see this as weakness or failure. I see it as where I am right now. A place shaped by fear, yes, but also by exhaustion, by caution, by a deep desire not to make things worse when I already feel stretched thin. So, I remain here, holding both truths at once, letting neither one resolve. Not because I think this is sustainable forever, but because it's what I'm capable of right now. And acknowledging that feels more honest than forcing myself into a step I'm not ready to take. The stalemate doesn't feel like peace. It doesn't feel like progress. It feels like waiting. Waiting for strength. Waiting for clarity. Waiting for something to tip the balance. Until then, I stay suspended between knowing and not acting, carrying the weight of both, breathing carefully, still here, even when I don't yet know how to move forward. The exhaustion doesn't lift just because I've named it. It settles deeper, spreading into places I didn't realize were still holding tension. It shows up in small ways first, in the way my thoughts feel slower, in the way even simple decisions feel heavier than they should. Nothing collapses. Nothing explodes. Things just take more effort than they used to. I'm still functioning.

That's what makes it confusing. From the outside, I look fine enough. I show up. I respond. I participate. But inside, every day feels like I'm carrying something that never gets set down, something that quietly drains me without asking permission. The silence doesn't protect me from that cost. It just keeps it invisible. I notice how tired I am of managing myself. Of constantly checking in, constantly gauging whether I'm okay enough to keep going, constantly redirecting my thoughts before they wander too far. It's like I'm living with an internal supervisor who never clocks out, always alert, always watching, always ready to intervene. There's no rest in that, only maintenance.

The silence asks more of me than I expected. It asks me to be my own support system, my own monitor, my own safety net. It asks me to carry the full weight of this alone, without relief, without reassurance, without the option to lean. And even though I chose this, even though I understand why I'm here, the cost keeps adding up. I feel it in the quiet moments, when there's nothing to distract me from how depleted I am. I feel it when I think about the future and can't imagine it clearly, not because it's bleak, but because I'm too tired to picture anything beyond getting through the next stretch of time.

The horizon feels foggy, not threatening, just distant. I don't feel worse than before. I don't feel better either. I feel worn. That's what the silence does over time. It doesn't break you. It wears you down. Slowly. Subtly. It turns every day into something that requires effort without offering recovery. And the longer I stay here, the more I understand that this isn't neutral. It's taking something from me, even if it isn't taking me anywhere dramatic. I start to see how this could continue indefinitely.

How easy it would be to normalize this level of exhaustion, to accept it as the cost of staying quiet, to build a life around managing instead of living. That realization doesn't scare me the way panic does. It saddens me. It makes me feel like something important is slowly slipping out of reach while I'm busy holding everything together. I'm not in crisis. I'm not unraveling. I'm just tired of carrying this alone.

That thought sits with me, not as a demand, not as a call to action, but as a quiet truth I can't ignore anymore. The cost of silence is becoming clearer, not all at once, but steadily, as exhaustion deepens without quieting the thoughts it was meant to protect me from. I stay where I am for now. Still silent. Still aware. Still suspended. But the weight feels different. Heavier. More persistent. And I can feel that this stalemate can't last forever, even if I don't yet know what will finally break it.

The door doesn't appear suddenly. It's been there the whole time. I just can't avoid seeing it anymore. Knowing help exists used to feel abstract, something I could acknowledge without engaging. Now it feels physical, like I'm standing directly in front of it whether I want to be or not. I don't touch the handle. I just stand there, aware of how much space it takes up in my mind. I notice how often my thoughts drift toward it without permission, how frequently I find myself imagining what it would mean to open it and, just as quickly, imagining what it would cost.

The door doesn't ask anything of me. It doesn't pressure me. It just exists, solid and patient. That's what makes it impossible to ignore. I don't feel ready. I don't feel brave. I don't feel convinced. I feel exposed by the fact that the option is so clear now. There's no pretending I don't know what comes next. No claiming ignorance. No telling myself I'm just waiting for the right moment without knowing what that means. I'm standing here because exhaustion brought me here, not courage. The fear hasn't gone anywhere. If anything, it feels sharper now that the choice is more defined. I still fear being seen. Being misunderstood. Losing control. Being changed by the act of asking. All of that remains intact, heavy and real.

What's changed is that staying silent no longer feels invisible. It feels deliberate. It feels like something I'm actively maintaining. I don't feel pulled forward. I don't feel pushed back. I feel held in place by awareness. There's a strange vulnerability in that. In knowing exactly where you are and exactly what you're not doing. It strips away excuses. It leaves only honesty, and honesty doesn't offer comfort. It just tells the truth. I tell myself I'm allowed to stand here as long as I need to. That I don't owe anyone movement. That I don't owe anyone progress.

Even as I give myself that permission, I can feel the pressure of the moment. Not urgency, not panic, just the quiet understanding that standing still takes effort too. That not choosing is still a choice. That time keeps passing whether I move or not. The door stays closed. Not slammed shut. Not locked. Just closed, waiting. And I stay on my side of it, aware of its presence in a way that feels permanent now.

I can't pretend I don't see it. I can't pretend it isn't part of my reality anymore. So, I stand there, suspended between fear and exhaustion, knowing I'm not ready to open the door, but also knowing I can't walk away from it the way I used to. The space between those two truths feels narrow and heavy, like a corridor I must pass through slowly, one breath at a time. I don't move, but I don't turn away either.

There's no dramatic hesitation, no last-minute surge of courage or fear. I just don't move. I stay exactly where I am, aware of the door, aware of what's on the other side of it, aware of myself standing here with no clear reason to step forward and no way to pretend I haven't arrived at this place. That stillness feels intentional. Not strong. Not decisive. Just honest.

I know what it would mean to open it. I know what it would cost me. I also know what staying here is costing me too. Both truths exist at the same time, pressing against each other without resolving. And instead of forcing an answer, I let that tension exist. I let myself remain in the middle of it. There's something grounding about not pretending anymore.

I'm not telling myself I'll ask for help tomorrow. I'm not promising myself anything I can't follow through on. I'm simply acknowledging where I am right now. Exhausted. Afraid. Aware. Still here. That feels more real than any plan I could make in this moment. I don't feel like I've failed. That's important. I don't see this as weakness or avoidance. I see it as where I am, shaped by everything I've carried up to this point.

The fear, the exhaustion, the need for control, the desire to protect myself from more than I think I can handle. All of it makes sense, even if it isn't sustainable forever. I'm standing at the door, not reaching out, not turning away. And maybe that's its own kind of truth. This chapter doesn't end with help. It doesn't end with relief.

It doesn't end with answers. It ends with me still breathing, still choosing to stay, still living inside a decision I haven't made yet. The suspension isn't comfortable, but it's honest. It reflects the reality of where I am better than any neat resolution ever could. I don't know when the door will open. I don't know what will finally push me to move. All I know is that I see it now. I can't unsee it. And even in my refusal, even in my fear, even in my exhaustion, I'm still here, standing on this side of it, carrying the weight of knowing and not acting at the same time. That's where this chapter ends. Not with action. Not with change. But with the truth of quiet suspension, and the reality that sometimes-surviving means standing still longer than anyone expects, including yourself.

Chapter 10

Learning New Rules – How life changed

I stop waiting for anxiety and depression to leave. That's the first rule, even if I don't say it that clearly at first. It settles in gradually, through experience more than thought, through the realization that no matter how much I analyze, manage, or hope, they're still here. Not louder. Not quieter. Just present in the background of my life, like weather, I can't control. For a long time, I believed life would restart once they were gone. That there would be a moment where things would lift and I'd finally step back into myself the way I used to be. I carried that idea quietly, letting it shape how I measured my days, how I judged my progress, how I decided whether I was doing okay or not. Now that idea feels unrealistic. Not because I've given up, but because I've paid attention. Anxiety and depression haven't disappeared just because I hit bottom. They didn't leave because I stood at the door to help and didn't open it.

They didn't vanish because I survived something hard. They stayed, steady, familiar, and part of the landscape now. And something in me shifts when I accept that, not in a defeated way, but in a grounding way. Like I stop wasting energy on the constant question of when will this end and start asking a quieter one instead: how do I live with this here? That question doesn't scare me the way it used to. I don't feel dramatic about it. I don't feel hopeless. I feel realistic. This is my mind right now. This is my body right now. Waiting for a version of myself that doesn't have anxiety or depression feels like waiting for permission to live, and I'm too tired to keep postponing my own existence. So, I stay. Not because it's easy. Not because I feel strong. Because life is still happening, whether I feel ready for it or not, and something in me recognizes that my presence matters even when I'm struggling. Even when I'm tired. Even when my thoughts aren't kind. Even when I don't feel like the version of myself, I miss. Anxiety and depression don't disappear when I accept them. They don't soften or apologize for staying. But they also don't get to decide whether I belong here. That feels important to recognize, even if it doesn't come with relief. Life doesn't suddenly feel lighter. It just feels more honest. I stop treating my existence like something conditional, like something I earn only on good days or stable days or days when I feel okay enough. I don't need to be free of this to be allowed to exist. I don't need to be fixed to justify staying. That realization doesn't solve anything. But it gives me something solid to stand on. This is the new rule, even if I don't fully understand how to live by it yet: anxiety and depression may be part of my life, but they are not the reason my life stops. They don't get the final say on whether I show up, whether I stay, whether I continue to take up space in a world that's still moving. I don't feel victorious saying that, I feel steady. For now, steadiness is enough to keep me here, learning how to live differently instead of waiting to feel different.

Letting go of the idea that life starts *after this* happens slowly. It doesn't arrive as a decision or a moment of clarity. It shows up in the way I stop telling myself to just get through today so I can really live tomorrow. In the way tomorrow stops feeling like a finish line and starts feeling like another day I'm already inside. For a long time, I measured everything against a future version of myself. The one who wasn't anxious. The one who didn't feel heavy. The one who woke up without immediately checking in with their own mind. I kept believing that version was waiting somewhere ahead of me, and that I just needed to endure long enough to reach them. That belief kept me going, but it also kept me absent. I realize how much of my life I've been postponing, how often I've treated the present like something to survive rather than inhabit. Even on days that weren't terrible, I was still holding back, still saving myself for a time when things would feel easier, lighter, more manageable. I lived with one foot in the now and one foot in an imagined future where everything finally made sense, but that future never arrived. Anxiety and depression stayed. Life kept happening anyway. And somewhere along the way, the waiting started to feel heavier than the living. I got tired of telling myself this doesn't count yet, of acting like my life was on hold until my mind cooperated. There's a quiet defiance in letting that go. Not rebellion. Not anger. Just a refusal to keep putting my life on pause. I don't need permission from my mental state to exist fully in the days I'm given. I don't need to feel good to show up. I don't need certainty to participate in my own life.

This doesn't mean I suddenly feel present all the time. I still drift. I still struggle. I still have days where everything feels distant and effortful. But I stop framing those days as obstacles to living and start recognizing them as part of it. Life isn't waiting for me to catch up. That realization lands softly but firmly. It doesn't demand anything from me. It just asks me to stop disappearing from my own story while I wait to feel better. It asks me to stay, even imperfectly, even cautiously, even with the noise still there. I don't romanticize this shift. It doesn't feel brave. It feels practical. Like choosing to live inside reality instead of constantly reaching for a version of it that may never come. And there's relief in that, not the kind that lifts everything, but the kind that steadies you enough to keep moving. I stop asking when this will be over and I start asking how I move through today. That question feels smaller, more manageable. It keeps me grounded in what's actually happening instead of what I wish would happen. It doesn't promise happiness. It just offers presence, and right now, presence feels like progress. Letting go of "after this" doesn't mean giving up hope. It means redefining it. Hope stops being about a future without anxiety or depression and starts being about finding ways to live meaningfully with them still here. And that shift, quiet as it is, changes how I show up to my days. Not dramatically. Not perfectly. But enough that life starts to feel less like something I'm waiting for and more like something I'm already inside.

Staying in life starts to feel like something I choose, not something that just happens because I haven't left yet. That distinction matters more than I expect it to. There's a difference between existing by momentum and deciding, quietly, that I'm going to remain present even when it would be easier to check out emotionally. I notice it in small moments first. In the way I don't rush through the day just to get it over with. In the way I let myself sit with discomfort without immediately searching for an exit. In the way I stop treating every hard feeling like evidence that something is wrong and start seeing it as information instead. Staying doesn't mean enjoying any of this. It just means I'm here for it. There's a gentle defiance in that choice. Not loud. Not dramatic. Just a steady refusal to disappear from my own life again. I don't announce it to myself. I don't frame it as courage. I just keep showing up in small, imperfect ways, even when anxiety tightens my chest or depression dulls everything around me. Some days, staying feels easy enough. Other days, it feels deliberate, like I'm reminding myself over and over that I'm allowed to be here even when I don't feel okay. I don't need to justify my presence. I don't need to earn it by feeling better or functioning better or thinking better.

That realization changes how I relate to myself. I stop pushing so hard against what I feel. I stop treating my inner world like an obstacle I need to overcome before I'm allowed to live. Anxiety and depression don't disappear when I do this, but they stop being the sole focus. They become part of the experience instead of the definition of it. Staying doesn't fix my thoughts. It steadies my footing. I realize that choosing to stay isn't about commitment to some imagined future. It's about committing to this moment, and then the next one, without demanding that they feel different first. It's about allowing myself to take up space in my own life, even when I feel unsure or heavy or disconnected. There's a quiet power in that. Not power over my mind. Not power over my symptoms. Power over the decision to remain present. To not let my life slip past me while I'm waiting for my internal experience to change. To acknowledge that this is my life right now, and I'm still part of it, even on days when I don't feel fully engaged. I don't frame this as strength. I frame it as honesty. Honesty about what I'm capable of. Honesty about what I'm not. Honesty about the fact that staying doesn't require certainty or comfort, just a willingness to be here despite the noise. And that willingness, even when it's quiet and shaky, feels like a new kind of rule I'm learning to live by. I stay. Not because I know where this is going. Not because I feel ready. Because my presence still matters, even when my mind tells me otherwise. And choosing to believe that, again and again, becomes the way I move forward now, one day at a time, without waiting to feel different first.

Life doesn't slow down just because I've changed the way I'm thinking about it. It keeps moving at the same pace, asking the same things of me, expecting the same level of participation. The difference now is that I'm no longer pretending I can meet those expectations the way I used to. I feel that shift immediately. In the way I approach my days with more caution. In the way I don't stack commitments on top of each other without thinking through the cost. In the way I pay attention to how my body reacts instead of pushing through automatically. The old rule was to keep up no matter what. The new one is quieter and less impressive: move in a way that lets you stay. I don't rush the mornings the same way anymore. Not because I've found peace or balance, but because I've learned what happens when I ignore the warning signs. The tightness in my chest. The fog in my head. The sense that I'm pushing myself into a place I won't recover from easily. I move slower now, not as a luxury, but as a necessity. Life still demands things from me. Work still exists. Relationships still require presence. Responsibilities don't disappear just because I've reached a new understanding. But I start interacting with those demands differently. I don't automatically say yes. I don't assume I should be able to handle everything. I stop measuring myself by how much I can endure. That change feels uncomfortable. It goes against everything I've been taught about productivity and strength and pushing through.

There's guilt in it at first, a sense that I'm doing something wrong by not operating at full capacity. But the guilt softens when I notice the alternative. When I notice how much worse things get when I ignore my limits. Life didn't pause for me, I had to change how I moved through it. That realization doesn't make things easier. It makes them more deliberate. Every choice carries weight now. Every yes comes with a calculation. Every no comes with explanation, sometimes only to me, sometimes to others. I don't feel carefree. I feel aware. There's loss in that awareness. I miss the version of myself who didn't have to think this much about existing. Who could take on more without consequence. Who didn't need to plan recovery time or anticipate emotional fallout. That grief sits quietly alongside the acceptance, reminding me that learning new rules also means letting go of old freedoms. But there's something stabilizing in this shift too. I'm no longer constantly surprised by my own limits. I'm no longer pretending they don't exist. I start building my days around what I can actually manage instead of what I think I should be able to manage. That doesn't feel like giving up. It feels like staying in the game. Life keeps moving.

And instead of trying to outrun it, I start walking at a pace that lets me stay alongside it, even when it feels uncomfortable, even when it feels slower than I want, even when it doesn't look like the life I imagined for myself before all of this. This isn't growth the way people talk about growth. It's adaptation, and adaptation, right now, is what keeps me here. A good day doesn't mean what it used to anymore. It used to mean productivity. Momentum. Energy. Checking things off a list and feeling like I earned the right to rest afterward. A good day used to be something you could point to and explain, something visible, something that made sense to other people. Now it's quieter than that. A good day is a day I don't spiral. A day I notice the anxiety without letting it drive everything. A day I feel the heaviness and still get out of bed anyway. Some days, a good day is just one where nothing gets worse.

That shift takes time to accept. There's a part of me that resists it, that wants more, that misses the satisfaction of doing and achieving and feeling capable in a way that doesn't require so much internal negotiation. I grieve that version of "good" even as I learn to redefine it. I start measuring my days differently. Not by what I accomplish, but by how I treat myself while I'm here. By whether I listened when my body asked me to slow down. By whether I let myself rest without guilt. By whether I stayed present instead of dissociating through the hours just to get them over with. Some days, I don't do much at all. And that used to feel like failure. Now it feels like information. It tells me where my limits are that day, what kind of day it is, what's realistic instead of what's expected. I stop forcing meaning into my days and start allowing them to be what they are. There's relief in that. Not excitement. Not joy. Relief.

Relief from constantly judging myself for not being who I used to be. Relief from comparing this version of my life to one that no longer exists. Relief from the exhausting belief that every day needs to prove something. A good day can be small now. It can be quiet. It can be uneventful. It can be a day where I show up halfway and forgive myself for the other half. A day where I eat, sleep, breathe, and don't ask anything more of myself than that. Those days don't look impressive, but they keep me grounded, and right now, being grounded matters more than being impressive ever did. I don't celebrate these days loudly. I don't announce them. I just notice them. I notice how redefining "good" lowers the pressure I put on myself. How it creates space to exist without constantly striving for a version of life that feels out of reach. How it lets me stay instead of burn out trying to prove I'm okay. This new definition doesn't erase the hard days. It just gives me a way to live through them without feeling like every struggle is a personal failure. It gives me permission to keep going at a pace that doesn't punish me for being human. A good day isn't about feeling better. It's about staying and learning that changes everything about how I move through my life now, one quiet day at a time.

The noise never fully goes away. Anxiety hums in the background, steady and familiar, while depression dulls the edges of things I used to feel more sharply. For a long time, I treated that noise like an enemy, something I had to fight or silence before I could move forward. Now, I stop fighting it so aggressively. Not because I've accepted it in some peaceful way, Because fighting it was exhausting me. I start learning how to live with the noise instead of constantly reacting to it. I notice it without immediately trying to fix it. I let anxious thoughts pass through without chasing every one of them to its conclusion. I let the heaviness exist without turning it into a verdict about my life. That shift is subtle. It doesn't look like progress from the outside. Inside, it feels like creating a little space between me and my thoughts, just enough to breathe. The noise is still there, but it's no longer the only thing I hear. Life continues alongside it, quieter, slower, but still present. Some days, the noise is louder. On those days, I don't try to overpower it. I lower my expectations. I move carefully. I don't demand clarity or motivation from myself. I let the day be what it is without turning it into proof that I'm backsliding or failing. That restraint feels unfamiliar. I was used to pushing back, arguing with my mind, trying to win against something that didn't play by rules. Now I'm learning that coexistence takes less energy than constant resistance. It doesn't make me feel better. It makes me feel less depleted. I start noticing moments that exist outside the noise. Small things. A sense of routine. A familiar place.

A moment where my attention drifts just long enough to remind me that my mind isn't the only thing happening in the world. Those moments don't erase the anxiety or the depression. They sit beside them, proof that life is still unfolding even when my internal experience is loud. I don't romanticize this. Living alongside the noise isn't graceful. It's messy and uneven and sometimes frustrating. There are days when I miss the simplicity of believing I could think my way out of this, days when acceptance feels like giving up. But I remind myself that I'm not surrendering. I'm adapting. The noise doesn't get to be the center of everything anymore. It's part of my experience, not the definition of it. I carry it with me as I move through my days, learning when to listen to it and when to let it exist without reaction. That balance isn't consistent. It changes day to day, sometimes hour to hour. And that's okay. I'm not trying to eliminate the noise anymore. I'm trying to live my life with it present, without letting it consume every thought, every moment, every decision. That effort doesn't feel heroic. It feels necessary. And slowly, almost without noticing, I realize that life doesn't have to be silent to be livable. It just has to leave enough room for me to stay.

Somewhere along the way, I start separating who I am from what I'm experiencing. Not cleanly. Not all at once. Just enough to notice the difference. Anxiety and depression are present, sometimes loud, sometimes quiet, but they aren't the sum of me. They don't get to narrate my entire existence anymore. For a long time, everything filtered through them. Every reaction felt suspicious. Every low moment felt like confirmation. Every anxious thought felt like a warning I had to take seriously. I didn't just *have* anxiety and depression — I *was* them. They shaped how I talked about myself, how I explained my limits, how I understood my place in the world. That starts to loosen. Not because the symptoms disappear, but because I stop letting them define my identity. I notice that there are parts of me that exist even when the noise is loud. Parts that make choices. Parts that care. Parts that keep showing up even when my mind is telling me to retreat. I'm still here underneath all of it. That realization feels grounding in a way I didn't expect. It doesn't minimize what I'm dealing with. It doesn't pretend this is easy. It just creates space for the truth that I am more than my worst thoughts, more than my most exhausted moments, more than the days when everything feels heavy. Some days, that distinction feels clear. Other days, it blurs again, and I have to remind myself gently that experiencing something doesn't mean becoming it.

Anxiety can speak without being right. Depression can exist without being prophetic. I don't have to take everything my mind offers me as fact. That doesn't mean I ignore it, it means I contextualize it. I start asking quieter questions. Is this thought coming from fear, or from reality? Is this heaviness information, or is it just a feeling passing through? I don't interrogate myself harshly. I just pause long enough to remember that I'm allowed to exist beyond what my mind is producing in that moment. There's relief in that separation. Not relief from symptoms, but relief from identification. I don't collapse into every anxious spike anymore. I don't see every low mood as evidence that I'm broken or failing. I recognize patterns without turning them into identities. I am not my anxiety. I am not my depression. I am someone who lives with them, navigates around them, learns how to function alongside them. That distinction gives me a little breathing room, a little dignity back, a little sense of self that doesn't disappear just because my mind is loud. I still struggle. I still have hard days. But I'm no longer reducing myself to my hardest moments. I'm learning to hold them without letting them swallow everything else I am. And that shift, quiet as it is, changes how I see myself moving forward. I'm not defined by what I carry. I'm defined by the fact that I'm still here, carrying it.

Choosing to exist doesn't always feel like a choice that makes sense. It isn't comforting. It isn't rewarding. A lot of the time, it feels inconvenient, like something I commit to without getting anything immediate in return. And yet, I keep choosing it, quietly, daily, without ceremony. Comfort stops being the goal. For a long time, I believed the point of getting through this was to feel better, to feel lighter, to feel at ease again. When that didn't happen, I felt like I was doing something wrong. Now I understand that comfort isn't always available, and waiting for it was keeping me from living at all. Some days are uncomfortable from the moment I wake up. My thoughts are heavy. My body feels resistant. My patience wears thin quickly. On those days, choosing to stay doesn't feel noble. It feels practical. Like deciding to remain upright in rough weather instead of waiting for the storm to pass before stepping outside.

I don't choose existence because it feels good. I choose it because disappearing, even emotionally, costs me more in the long run. I've learned that checking out doesn't bring relief, it just delays the weight and makes it heavier when it returns. Staying present, even when it's uncomfortable, keeps me connected to something real. That choice happens in small moments. When I resist the urge to isolate completely. When I stay in a room even though I want to leave. When I let a difficult feeling exist without immediately numbing it or running from it. None of that feels satisfying in the moment. It feels like endurance. It feels like tolerance. It feels like choosing the harder option when there isn't a clearly easier one.

There are days when comfort does show up unexpectedly. Not as happiness, but as neutrality. A moment where the noise softens just enough for me to notice something else. Those moments don't feel like rewards for choosing to stay. They feel like reminders that life still has texture, even when my internal experience is rough. I stopped chasing those moments. I stopped measuring my days by how comfortable they feel and start measuring them by whether I stayed engaged at all. Whether I remained present. Whether I allowed myself to exist inside discomfort without turning it into something catastrophic. Choosing existence becomes quieter over time. It stops feeling like a decision and starts feeling like a rhythm. Something I return to automatically, even on days when my mind argues against it. I don't need to convince myself that this will pay off. I just need to keep showing up. Comfort comes and goes.

Existence stays. And learning to prioritize the one over the other doesn't make life easier. It makes it real. It gives me a way to keep living without waiting for conditions that may never fully arrive. It teaches me that I don't need to feel good to belong here. I can stay even when it's uncomfortable. I can stay even when it's hard. That rule doesn't promise relief. It promises continuity. And right now, continuity is what keeps me grounded, moving forward in a life that's imperfect but still mine. The hard days don't disappear just because I've learned how to stay. They come back quietly, sometimes without warning, slipping into my routine like they never left. The difference now isn't in how they feel. It's in what they mean. Before, a bad day felt like proof. Proof that I wasn't getting better. Proof that nothing had changed. Proof that all the work I thought I was doing was pointless. A single hard day could undo weeks in my mind, could convince me that everything was fragile, temporary, conditional. I treated setbacks like verdicts instead of moments. Now, I don't let them rewrite the whole story. That doesn't mean they hurt less. Anxiety still tightens my chest. Depression still flattens things I wish I could feel more deeply. I still wake up some mornings already tired, already bracing myself for a day that feels heavier than it should. The sensations are familiar. The thoughts still try to pull me under. But they don't carry the same authority. A hard day doesn't tell me who I am anymore. It doesn't tell me where I'm headed. It doesn't erase the fact that I stayed yesterday or that I'll likely stay again tomorrow. It's just a day. A difficult one, yes, but not a prophecy. That shift matters more than I realized it would. I stop panicking when things feel bad again. I stop rushing to interpret the discomfort. I don't immediately assume I've failed or slipped backward. I let the day be what it is without demanding it mean something larger. Some days still feel long.

Time stretches. Motivation disappears. Everything feels heavier to carry. On those days, I don't reach for lessons or silver linings. I don't tell myself this is making me stronger. I just get through the hours as gently as I can, reminding myself that surviving a hard day is still surviving. Progress doesn't feel linear anymore. It feels layered. Like I'm building something underneath the bad days instead of on top of good ones. The foundation doesn't crack just because a day is hard. It holds, quietly, even when everything above it feels unsteady. That realization brings a kind of calm. Not peace. Not confidence. Calm. Calm in knowing that difficulty doesn't automatically mean danger. That discomfort doesn't require immediate correction. That I can have a bad day without it undoing the fact that I've learned how to stay. I don't rush to fix myself anymore. I let the hard days pass through me the way weather does, uncomfortable but temporary. I don't make promises about tomorrow. I don't catastrophize the future. I just stay present long enough for the day to end, trusting that one day doesn't define my entire life. Hard days still come. They always will. But they no longer get to decide whether everything else counts. They're part of the landscape now, not the whole terrain. And learning that gives me a steadiness I didn't have before, a sense that I can keep going even when things feel rough again. I stay. Even on the hard days. Especially on the hard days.

Strength doesn't look the way I was taught it would. It doesn't look like pushing harder or ignoring what hurts or proving that I can handle more than I should. I spent a long time believing that strength meant endurance at any cost, that if I could just keep going without breaking, that counted as success. Now I see how much that version of strength took from me. The strength I'm learning now is quieter. It shows up when I stop before I'm depleted instead of after. When I admit I'm tired without turning that into shame. When I choose not to explain myself to people who don't need an explanation. None of that looks impressive. None of it earns praise. But it keeps me here. I don't override myself the way I used to. I pay attention when my body tightens, when my thoughts speed up, when the heaviness settles in earlier than expected. I don't always know what to do with those signals, but I don't ignore them anymore. Listening feels like an act of respect, even when I don't fully understand what I'm being asked for.

There's resistance in that. A part of me still wants to push, to prove that I'm capable, to return to the version of myself who didn't need so many accommodations. That part doesn't disappear just because I've learned new rules. It shows up often, questioning whether I'm doing enough, whether I'm letting this define me too much. I don't argue with it harshly. I acknowledge it and keep going anyway, choosing sustainability over approval. Choosing to stay instead of burning out. That choice feels like strength now, even if it doesn't look like it from the outside. Some days, strength looks like rest. Other days, it looks like doing the bare minimum and letting that be enough. It looks like walking away before I'm overwhelmed instead of staying until I collapse. It looks like adjusting expectations instead of punishing myself for not meeting them. That shift changes how I move through my life. I stop measuring myself against who I used to be. I stop chasing a standard that doesn't fit my reality anymore. I start building something quieter, something that doesn't rely on constant output or performance to feel valid. This kind of strength doesn't announce itself. It doesn't feel triumphant. It doesn't feel powerful. It feels steady. It feels grounded. It feels like choosing to protect my own ability to keep going, even when that means letting go of how things used to look. I'm still learning this. I still slip into old habits sometimes. I still push when I shouldn't. But more often now, I pause. I listen. I choose the option that lets me remain intact instead of the one that proves something to no one. Strength isn't about how much I can endure anymore. It's about how carefully I can live without disappearing from myself again. And learning that redefines everything about what it means to keep going in a life that doesn't feel easy but still feels worth staying in.

Life doesn't stop offering moments just because anxiety and depression are still here. They arrive quietly, unannounced, slipping into days I wasn't expecting anything from. I don't always notice them right away. Sometimes they pass through before I realize what they were. They don't feel dramatic. They aren't breakthroughs or revelations. They're small, ordinary moments that exist alongside the noise without asking it to leave first. A familiar routine. A brief sense of focus. A moment where I catch myself engaged in something without checking in on my own mind every few seconds. Those moments surprise me. Not because they're rare, but because I stopped expecting them. For a long time, I believed I couldn't fully experience life while anxiety and depression were present, that everything meaningful had to wait until I felt better. Now I see that life keeps finding ways to show up anyway. I don't chase these moments. I don't hold onto them tightly or try to recreate them. I let them exist as they are, without turning them into evidence that I'm improving or failing. They're not measurements. They're reminders that my inner world isn't the only thing happening. Some days, the moments are subtle. A task completed without spiraling. A conversation that feels natural instead of forced. A stretch of time where I'm simply present, not monitoring, not bracing, not analyzing. Those moments don't erase the anxiety or depression.

They sit beside them, proof that my experience is layered, not singular. That realization softens something in me. I stop viewing my life as either suffering or healing. It's both. It always has been. I'm learning how to hold that complexity without trying to resolve it into something cleaner or easier to understand. I notice how these moments ground me. They don't make me feel happy in a conventional sense. They make me feel connected, like I'm still part of the world even when my mind is loud. They remind me that presence doesn't require silence, just attention. I don't build expectations around them. I let them come and go without assigning meaning. That restraint feels important. It keeps me from turning every good moment into pressure and every bad moment into panic. It lets life breathe around me instead of being filtered entirely through my internal state. These moments don't save me. But they anchor me. They give shape to my days, texture to my experience, proof that I'm still living even when things feel heavy. And learning to notice them without clinging to them becomes part of the new rules I'm building, rules that allow life to exist alongside anxiety and depression without waiting for them to disappear first. I don't need life to be perfect to be present in it. I just need to be here long enough to notice that it's still happening.

Giving myself permission to take up space again feels unfamiliar. Not because I don't want to, but because I've spent so long shrinking without realizing it. I learned how to be quieter, easier, less noticeable, believing that making myself smaller would make everything more manageable. It didn't. It just made me disappear from my own life. Taking up space doesn't mean demanding attention or asserting myself loudly. It means allowing myself to exist fully in the room without apologizing for it. It means not pulling back automatically when I feel heavy or tired or uncertain. It means trusting that my presence doesn't need justification. That's harder than it sounds. There's a reflex to minimize. To assume I'm too much. To step back before anyone asks me to. Those instincts run deep, shaped by fear and exhaustion and the belief that my struggles make me inconvenient. Undoing that takes awareness I didn't know I had. I start small. I let myself speak when I have something to say instead of waiting to be invited. I stay in conversations instead of fading out halfway through. I allow myself to have opinions, preferences, needs, even when they feel messy or unpolished. None of this feels natural yet. It feels like learning a language I forgot how to speak. There's discomfort in occupying space.

A quiet worry that I'm asking for too much, that my presence will be felt in ways I can't control. But there's also something grounding about it. Something steadying. Each time I resist the urge to shrink, I feel a little more anchored in my own body, a little less like I'm floating through my days unseen. I remind myself that existing isn't a burden. That I don't have to earn my place by being easy or unaffected or consistently okay. I don't owe the world a version of myself that feels convenient. I owe myself honesty, and honesty means allowing myself to show up as I am, not as who I think I should be. This permission doesn't arrive all at once. Some days, I still pull back. Some days, I still disappear a little when things feel overwhelming. But more often now, I notice it happening and choose differently. I stay. I speak. I let myself be present even when it feels uncomfortable. Taking up space doesn't fix anything. It doesn't quiet my mind or lift the heaviness. But it reconnects me to my life in a way shrinking never did. It reminds me that I'm allowed to be here fully, not conditionally, not quietly tucked away in the background. I don't need to be easy to deserve space. I just need to be here. And learning to believe that, even on days when it feels undeserved, becomes another rule I carry with me, one that keeps me grounded in a life that's imperfect, ongoing, and still mine.

Staying starts to feel like enough. Not in a way that settles everything or makes life feel complete, but in a way that quiets the constant pressure to become something else before I'm allowed to exist. I stop treating staying as the bare minimum and start recognizing it as an achievement in itself, even if no one else sees it that way. For a long time, I believed survival didn't count unless it led somewhere. Unless it turned into growth, or healing, or a story that made sense in retrospect. I needed my pain to justify itself, to prove it was moving me toward something better. Now I see how unfair that expectation was, how much weight I put on simply continuing to exist. Staying doesn't always lead somewhere obvious. Some days, it just leads to the next day. And that has to be enough. I don't demand meaning from every moment anymore. I don't ask my life to explain itself. I let it unfold without insisting that it turn into something inspirational. There's relief in lowering that bar. Not because I don't care about my life, but because I care about it enough to stop forcing it into a shape it can't hold right now. Staying is work. It takes energy. It takes intention. It takes resilience I don't always recognize in myself. I stop minimizing that. I stop telling myself that just being here doesn't count because I'm not thriving or improving fast enough. I stop dismissing the effort it takes to remain engaged with a life that feels heavy more often than it feels light. Staying isn't passive. It's an active choice I make repeatedly, even when it feels small, even when it feels unimpressive. It's choosing not to withdraw completely. Choosing not to disappear. Choosing to keep showing up in whatever capacity I have that day. I don't need my life to look a certain way to validate that choice. I don't need proof that this will all make sense later. I don't need reassurance that staying will eventually pay off. I just need to recognize that staying itself has value, even when everything else feels uncertain.

That realization doesn't change my circumstances. But it changes how I see myself inside them. I stop seeing myself as someone who is failing to move forward and start seeing myself as someone who is actively remaining present in the face of difficulty. That matters. It gives me dignity in moments that used to feel empty. It gives weight to days that might otherwise blur together. It gives me permission to exist without constantly striving for something more. Staying is enough for now. Not forever. Not as a final destination. But as a rule that allows me to keep living without turning my life into a constant evaluation of progress. And learning to accept that brings a steadiness I didn't know I was allowed to feel.

The rules don't come with certainty. They don't promise anything beyond what they are. I don't suddenly feel confident about the future or clear about where I'm headed. What I feel instead is steadier, quieter, less demanding. I carry these rules forward without knowing exactly how they'll hold up. Some days they feel solid. Other days they feel fragile, like something I could forget if I'm not paying attention. I don't assume they'll protect me from hard moments. I don't believe they'll prevent anxiety or depression from flaring up again. I just trust that they give me something to return to when things get heavy. That trust feels new. I stop expecting certainty from myself. I stop demanding that I know how this ends before I allow myself to continue. Uncertainty doesn't feel like a threat anymore. It feels like the natural state of things, something I can move through instead of something I need to resolve.

I don't have answers. I don't have guarantees. I have awareness. Awareness of my limits. Awareness of what keeps me grounded. Awareness of the fact that I can live without clarity and still be present.

That realization loosens something in me that used to tighten whenever I thought too far ahead. I learn to carry the unknown without panicking. Not gracefully. Not consistently. But with more patience than before. I don't try to map out my life in detail anymore. I focus on staying connected to it instead. On remaining responsive instead of predictive. On letting things unfold without demanding that they make sense immediately. These rules aren't rigid. They bend. They adapt. They change depending on the day, the moment, the energy I have available. That flexibility matters. It keeps me from turning survival into another performance I have to get right. I don't need certainty to keep going. I just need enough steadiness to take the next step when it's available, and enough compassion to pause when it isn't. I learn that both are valid. Both are part of living. Carrying these rules forward doesn't feel like progress in the way people talk about progress. It feels like continuity. Like choosing to stay engaged with my life even when I don't know what it's becoming. And that feels honest. I don't pretend this is the end of anything. I don't frame it as a turning point that fixes what's been broken. I just acknowledge that I've learned how to live differently now, even in the absence of certainty. The future remains open, unclear, and unpromised. And for the first time in a long while, that doesn't scare me as much as it used to. It just feels like the space where life happens, and I'm still here, willing to move through it as I am.

The rules don't announce themselves as something permanent. They don't arrive with confidence or certainty or the feeling that I've finally figured something out. They exist quietly in the background of my life now, shaping how I move through my days without demanding attention. I don't wake up thinking about them. I notice them in hindsight, in the way I pause instead of push, in the way I stay present instead of waiting for things to feel different, in the way I choose to remain even when comfort isn't available. They show up not as thoughts, but as behavior, as instinct, as a quieter way of being. This chapter doesn't end with clarity. It ends with continuation. I'm still learning. Still adjusting. Still carrying anxiety and depression with me as part of my experience. They haven't left. They haven't softened. But they no longer get to decide whether my life moves forward or not. That feels important to acknowledge. Not as victory. Not as healing. As commitment. A commitment to stay inside my life, even when it's messy, even when it's uncomfortable, even when it doesn't look the way I thought it would. I don't promise myself that this will get easier.

I don't promise myself that the noise will fade. I just promise myself that I won't disappear from my own story again. That promise feels quiet and firm. It doesn't ask for belief. It doesn't require optimism. It simply exists, grounded in everything I've learned so far. Anxiety and depression may remain, but so do I. That balance feels fragile and real and honest in a way I trust. This is the new way forward. Not defined by absence of pain. Not defined by certainty. Defined by presence. I don't need to know where this leads to keep going. I don't need to understand everything to remain engaged. I just need to keep choosing to live under these rules, one day at a time, allowing life to unfold without waiting for it to feel different first. Chapter Ten doesn't close with an answer. It closes with me still here, still breathing, still learning how to live in a world that hasn't changed, with a mind that still struggles, and a life that remains worth staying in anyway. And for now, that's enough to carry forward.

Chapter 11

Small Wins – Celebrating surviving

There was a time when I didn't have to worry throughout the day. I didn't wake up checking my body or scanning my thoughts for signs of what might go wrong. I didn't live inside a constant awareness of myself. Life moved forward without commentary, without preparation, without that low-level tension sitting quietly in the background. Back then, worry made sense. It showed up when something was actually wrong, when there was a real reason for it to exist. It had edges. It came and went. It didn't follow me into every quiet moment or linger when nothing was happening. I didn't think about thinking. I didn't measure how I felt before deciding what I could handle. I just moved through the day without realizing how rare that would become. I didn't know I would miss that version of living. The shift didn't happen all at once. There wasn't a single moment where worry arrived and never left. It crept in slowly, disguised as caution at first, then concern, then something more constant. One day I realized I wasn't reacting anymore — I was anticipating.

Running through possibilities before anything had even happened. Preparing for outcomes I couldn't see but felt responsible for anyway. Now worry doesn't interrupt my life. It lives inside it. It's there when I wake up, before I've even decided how the day will go. It's there in the background as I move through ordinary moments, not loud enough to stop me, but persistent enough to be felt. A hum. A static.

Something I've learned to live with even though I never chose it. At first, that terrified me. I thought the constant presence of worry meant something was deeply wrong. That if my mind never fully relaxed, it must be because danger was coming or because I was failing to cope. I treated the noise like a problem that needed to be solved, something I had to eliminate before I could feel safe again. I didn't realize how much energy that fight was taking. Eventually, without planning to, I stopped reacting to the worry. Not because it disappeared, but because reacting to it every moment became unsustainable. I still noticed it. I still felt it. But instead of engaging every thought, I started carrying it. Letting it exist without asking it to explain itself. That didn't feel like progress at the time. It felt like resignation. Only later did I understand what was actually happening. I was adapting. Learning how to function with something present instead of waiting for it to leave. Learning how to move through a day knowing the "what ifs" would be there whether I invited them or not. I never had to do this.

Before, life didn't require this level of internal effort just to exist. Now it does. And the fact that I can still wake up, still show up, still move through hours with that background noise running quietly underneath everything — that matters, even if it doesn't look like much from the outside. This isn't a victory. It's not something I celebrate loudly or point to with pride. It's heavy. It's tiring. And some days I still wish for the ease I didn't know I had before. But there's also something validating in acknowledging that this adjustment takes effort, that living with constant worry isn't nothing. I didn't make the worry go away. I learned how to live with it there. And that — as unremarkable as it might sound — is the first small win. Not because it feels good, but because it allows me to keep going in a life that didn't stop just because my mind changed.

The worry doesn't announce itself anymore. It doesn't spike or scream or demand immediate attention the way it used to. It settles in quietly, like something permanent, like something I've learned not to question because questioning it doesn't change its presence. It's just there, woven into the fabric of my day. I don't wake up panicked. I wake up aware. Aware of myself. Of my thoughts. Of the way my body feels before I've even moved. The worry hums underneath everything, not loud enough to stop me, but constant enough that I never forget it's there. It's like background noise I've adjusted to, something I carry without reacting to every second. That adjustment didn't come from confidence. It came from repetition. From realizing that the noise didn't always mean something bad was about to happen. From watching days pass where the worry stayed present but nothing catastrophic followed. Slowly, my response changed. I stopped treating every anxious thought like a warning and started treating it like weather. Uncomfortable, persistent, but not always predictive. Some days it's easier to ignore. Other days it presses closer, harder to tune out, reminding me that it hasn't gone anywhere.

On those days, the effort it takes to function feels disproportionate to what I'm actually doing. Simple tasks require focus. Conversations require presence. Ordinary moments carry an extra layer of internal management that no one else can see. I don't explain that to people. From the outside, it looks like I'm just living my life. Inside, there's a constant calibration happening. Am I okay enough to keep going? Do I need to slow down? Can I push a little more, or is that going to cost me later? These questions run quietly in the background while I do things that used to feel automatic. This is where the small wins start to hide. Not in big accomplishments, but in the fact that I still show up at all. That I can move through a day with that noise present and not let it derail me completely. That I can feel the worry and still make choices, still engage, still exist without being consumed by it. There are moments when I catch myself doing something ordinary without thinking about the worry at all.

Those moments don't last long. They don't need to. Their existence is enough to remind me that my mind doesn't own every second of my life anymore. That even with the noise running underneath everything, I'm still capable of being present in small, unremarkable ways. I don't frame this as control. I haven't mastered anything. I haven't silenced my thoughts or trained myself into calm. I've just learned not to respond to every internal fluctuation as if it requires action. I've learned that sometimes the most effective thing I can do is let the noise exist without trying to negotiate with it. That restraint took time. It took trial and error and a lot of days that felt heavier than they needed to be. It took learning the difference between discomfort and danger, between worry and reality. And even now, I don't always get it right. I still engage when I don't need to. I still spiral sometimes. But more often than not, I keep going anyway.

The worry stays in the background, a constant companion I never invited but no longer fight aggressively. I don't like it. I don't appreciate it. I don't pretend it's useful. I just acknowledge it and keep living alongside it, one ordinary moment at a time. That doesn't feel like progress the way people usually talk about progress. It feels like endurance. Quiet, unseen endurance that doesn't get acknowledged because nothing dramatic is happening. But nothing dramatic happening is the point. The fact that I can live with the noise present, that I can function without constantly reacting to it, that I can let it exist without letting it take over — that's a win I never would have recognized before. Now I do. Not loudly. Not proudly. Just honestly. And that honesty makes it easier to keep going, even on days when the background noise feels heavier than usual, even when surviving doesn't look like much from the outside but takes everything I have on the inside.

Functioning starts to feel like work in a way it never did before. Not the kind of work you can point to or explain, but the kind that happens quietly in the background while everything else looks normal. From the outside, my days don't look that different. I wake up. I move through responsibilities. I respond when people talk to me. I do what needs to be done. Inside, there's an entirely different layer running at the same time. Every day requires a level of awareness I didn't used to need. I'm constantly adjusting, constantly checking in with myself without making it obvious. Am I pushing too hard? Am I disengaging? Am I okay enough to keep going, or do I need to slow down before I tip into something harder to manage? None of those questions stop the day. They just live alongside it, quietly shaping how I move.

That internal effort is invisible. No one sees the pause before I answer. No one notices the calculation behind a simple yes or no. No one feels the weight of staying present when my mind would rather drift somewhere quieter. From the outside, it looks like I'm just doing life. From the inside, it feels like I'm actively holding myself together while doing it. There's a strange loneliness in that. Not because I'm alone, but because the work I'm doing doesn't have language attached to it. I don't announce it. I don't explain it. I don't ask for recognition. I just carry it. And some days, that carrying takes more out of me than anything else I do. I used to judge myself for how tired I felt. I couldn't understand why ordinary days left me depleted, why doing what I'd always done suddenly felt heavier. I told myself I was being dramatic, lazy, weak. It took time to realize that functioning with constant internal noise requires energy, even when nothing is visibly wrong. That realization softens the way I see myself. I stop expecting the same output from a system that's working harder just to stay steady. I stop comparing my capacity now to a version of myself that didn't have to manage this extra layer. I start recognizing that getting through a day without spiraling, without shutting down, without disappearing emotionally is not nothing. Some days, functioning is all I do.

I don't excel. I don't feel engaged. I don't feel proud. I just exist within the day and make it to the other side. And that used to feel like failure. Now it feels like evidence of effort. Evidence that I'm still here, still participating, still choosing to move through life even when it requires more from me than it used to. There's no satisfaction attached to this. It doesn't feel good to need this much effort to do ordinary things. I don't celebrate it. I don't romanticize it. I just acknowledge it. I let myself see that there is work happening here, even if it doesn't come with visible results or external validation. Functioning anyway becomes its own kind of endurance. The kind that doesn't get noticed because nothing is falling apart. The kind that doesn't get praised because it looks like normalcy. The kind that only matters if you're the one doing it, day after day, carrying an internal weight that never fully sets down. I didn't used to count this as a win.

I thought wins had to look like improvement, or progress, or visible change. Now I understand that staying functional in the middle of something heavy is not a small thing. It's a quiet, ongoing effort that deserves recognition, even if that recognition comes only from me. I don't need my days to look impressive. I need them to be survivable. And learning to see functioning anyway as a form of strength — not the kind that conquers, but the kind that endures — changes how I move through my life. It gives me permission to be tired without being ashamed, to acknowledge effort without demanding results, to keep going without needing to prove that I'm okay. That shift doesn't make the work disappear. It just makes it visible. And seeing it for what it is makes it a little easier to keep carrying, one ordinary day at a time. Some of the most meaningful days now are the ones where nothing happens. Nothing breaks. Nothing spirals. Nothing forces me to stop and regroup. The day moves forward quietly, uneventfully, without asking anything dramatic from me. There was a time when I would have overlooked those days completely, dismissed them as neutral or unremarkable. Now I recognize how much effort it takes for them to exist. A day where nothing collapses is not empty. It's held together. I notice how much work goes into keeping things steady. The restraint it takes not to follow every anxious thought to its conclusion. The awareness required to catch myself before I disappear emotionally. The quiet decisions I make all day long to stay present enough, grounded enough, functional enough. None of that shows on the surface, but it shapes everything. These wins don't announce themselves. They don't come with relief or satisfaction. They don't feel like success. They feel like survival in its most ordinary form. A day where I ate. A day where I slept. A day where I showed up without unraveling. A day where the worry stayed in the background instead of taking over.

I used to minimize those days. I told myself they didn't count because nothing improved. Because I didn't feel better. Because I didn't learn anything new or reach some emotional milestone. I see now how unfair that was, how much pressure I put on myself to justify my existence with progress. Now I let those days stand on their own. I let a neutral day be enough. I let a day without crisis count as a win, even if it doesn't feel like one in the moment. I stop demanding meaning from every stretch of time and start appreciating the quiet continuity of just making it through. There's a strange humility in that. It asks me to notice what I would have ignored before. To acknowledge effort without needing it to turn into something impressive. To accept that surviving doesn't always look like movement or change.

Sometimes it looks like holding the line where I am. I don't talk about these wins with anyone. They're too small to explain. Too internal to describe without sounding dramatic. So, I carry them quietly, letting myself recognize them even if no one else ever does. That recognition matters more than I expected it to. It changes how I treat myself. I stop being so harsh about what I didn't do and start noticing what I managed not to lose. I stop framing every day as a test I either pass or fail. I start seeing it as a series of moments I navigated without falling apart, even when it would have been easier to check out. Some days, the win is simply staying regulated enough to keep going. Some days, it's not spiraling as far as I used to. Some days, it's catching myself sooner. Some days, it's choosing rest instead of punishment. None of these things feel celebratory. They feel necessary. And that's exactly why they matter. I don't need fireworks to validate my survival. I need honesty. Honesty about how much effort it takes to live this way. Honesty about how easy it would be to dismiss these days as nothing. Honesty about the fact that nothing falling apart is sometimes the biggest achievement I have. And learning to let that be enough gives my days a quiet kind of meaning. Not the kind you talk about. The kind you carry with you, unnoticed, steady, and real.

At some point, I stop arguing with myself about whether surviving is enough. I don't win that argument in a dramatic way. I just get tired of trying to convince myself that it doesn't count. The effort it takes to stay here, day after day, becomes impossible to ignore. I used to think survival was the starting line. Something you move past on the way to real progress. Something temporary. Something you don't linger in. Now I see how flawed that thinking was. For me, surviving hasn't been a phase. It's been the work. Quiet, repetitive, unremarkable work that doesn't lead to applause or clear milestones. Staying is not passive. It takes intention to wake up and move through a day knowing the worry will be there, knowing the noise won't fully quiet, knowing the effort will be invisible. It takes restraint not to disappear emotionally when it would be easier to check out. It takes patience to let life unfold without demanding that it feel better before I participate in it. I don't frame this as resilience anymore. That word feels too polished, too distant from the lived experience of it. What I'm doing isn't heroic. It's human. It's choosing to remain present in a life that feels heavier than it used to, without needing to justify that choice with improvement or transformation. Some days, staying looks like moving forward. Other days, it looks like holding still and not letting things get worse. Both count, even when neither feels satisfying. Both require something from me. Both keep me here. I stop minimizing that. I stop telling myself that just getting through a day doesn't matter because I didn't feel better, because nothing changed, because the worry didn't leave.

I stop treating my survival like an inconvenience or a placeholder for something more meaningful. This is meaningful, not because it's inspiring, not because it's impressive, because it's real. There's a quiet validation in allowing myself to acknowledge that staying alive, staying present, staying engaged in small, imperfect ways is not nothing. It's the foundation everything else rests on, whether anything else ever arrives or not. I don't need to celebrate this loudly. I don't need to turn it into a lesson or a victory story. I just need to let it count. To let myself see the truth of what I'm doing without dismissing it because it doesn't look the way I thought progress was supposed to look. Surviving isn't glamorous. It doesn't come with clarity or relief or a sense of arrival. It comes with repetition. With background noise. With days that blend together. And still, it matters. It matters because I'm still here, still choosing to live inside my life, even when it asks more of me than it used to. That's the win. Not the absence of struggle. Not the presence of hope. The fact that I stayed and letting that be enough doesn't make the weight disappear. It just gives me permission to keep carrying it without shame, without minimizing, without waiting for my life to turn into something else before I allow myself to value it. This chapter doesn't end with improvement. It ends with recognition.

Recognition that surviving is not small, that living with constant "what ifs" and continuing anyway is not nothing, that staying alive in a world that feels heavier than it once did is work worth acknowledging. I stayed. And for now, that counts.

Chapter 12

Relapses – When it comes back

It doesn't come back loudly. There's no spike, no rush, no panic that grabs me by the throat. What comes first is the heaviness. A weight that settles in my chest before I've had time to think about it, before I've decided how the day is going to go. It's familiar enough that I recognize it immediately, and that recognition alone is exhausting. Oh my god. Not again. Not today. The thought doesn't feel dramatic. It feels irritated. Tired. Like someone who's already done this too many times and knows exactly what it's going to require. The heaviness presses down, dull and slow, making everything feel harder before I've even moved. It doesn't demand attention. It just sits there, quietly insisting that today will take more effort than I have. I don't feel afraid when it happens. That surprises me every time. I used to associate relapse with panic, with spiraling, with the fear that everything was about to collapse. Now it feels different. Now it feels like disappointment mixed with fatigue. Like realizing I'm about to carry something heavy again when I was already tired. The heaviness isn't sadness exactly.

It's resistance. Resistance to getting out of bed. Resistance to engaging. Resistance to having to manage myself all over again. It's the feeling of my emotional world slowing down, thickening, becoming harder to move through. Everything feels weighted, like I'm walking through something denser than air. I know this feeling. That's the part that hits hardest. There's no confusion about what's happening. No curiosity. No surprise. My body knows it before my mind catches up, and that knowledge lands with a quiet frustration. I've been here before. I remember what this takes. I remember how much energy it costs just to function when this heaviness is present. And I don't want to do it again today. I feel the urge to check out early, to shrink my day before it even starts, to lower expectations not thoughtfully, but defensively. The thought creeps in that maybe I should just get through the bare minimum and call it done. That idea isn't dramatic. It's practical. It's survival trying to conserve energy. The hardest part is the timing. There's nothing obviously wrong. No trigger I can point to. No reason that makes this make sense. The heaviness just arrives, uninvited, dragging familiar weight behind it. And I'm left standing there, aware of what's happening, aware of what's coming, already tired at the thought of managing it. I don't tell myself I'm back at the beginning. Not yet. That comes later. Right now, all I feel is the burden of recognition. The frustration of knowing that even though I've learned new rules, even though I've adapted, even though I've survived worse, I still have to deal with this again, today. The heaviness settles in, patient and unmoved by my resistance. It doesn't care that I've been doing better. It doesn't care that I stayed. It doesn't care that I've learned how to live with this. It just exists, and I exist with it, staring down another day that suddenly feels heavier than it did a moment ago. This is how relapse announces itself now. Not as a crisis. Not as a breakdown. As a quiet, exhausting return of something I hoped I wouldn't have to carry today.

The heaviness doesn't stay contained. Once it settles in, it spreads, slow and deliberate, into everything else. My body starts moving differently before I consciously decide to adjust. My shoulders round forward. My steps feel heavier. Even breathing takes a little more effort, like the air has thickened overnight. Nothing hurts. Nothing is wrong. And yet everything feels harder. I notice how quickly my world narrows when this happens. The day ahead doesn't feel impossible, but it feels crowded, like every task is suddenly competing for energy I don't have. Things I would normally do without thinking now require a mental pause. A calculation. Can I handle this? Can I handle that? What can wait? What can't? This is the part that feels cruel. I haven't forgotten how to cope. I haven't lost awareness. If anything, I'm more aware than I used to be. I recognize the signs. I know what this is. And still, the weight presses down as if none of those matters. Knowing doesn't make it lighter. It just makes it familiar. There's a strange mix of competence and resentment here. I know how to get through a day like this. I know how to lower expectations, how to move slower, how to protect myself from spiraling too far. I've done this before. That knowledge should feel empowering. Instead, it feels exhausting. Like being handed a task I never volunteered for but am now expected to complete again. I move through the morning on autopilot. Not dissociated. Just dulled. The emotional heaviness acts like a filter, muting things that would normally register more clearly. Conversations feel distant. Time stretches.

The sense of effort never fully leaves. I'm doing the same things I always do, but they feel like they're happening under water. I keep thinking about how unfairly consistent this is. How the heaviness follows the same pattern every time. How my body recognizes it immediately. How there's no novelty to distract me from it anymore. It's not dramatic enough to demand help, not sharp enough to feel like a crisis, just persistent enough to drain me slowly. That's what makes relapse feel so discouraging now. It doesn't knock me over. It wears me down. It takes the steadiness I've built and tests it quietly, asking if I'm willing to carry this again without collapsing, without disappearing, without giving up the ground I fought to stand on. I feel irritation bubbling under the surface. Not at myself, but at the situation. At the fact that even when I've learned how to live with this, I don't get a break from it. At the reality that progress doesn't mean immunity. That knowing better doesn't always translate to feeling better. And still, the day moves forward. I don't stop living just because the heaviness is here. I move through it, adjusting without announcing it, carrying the weight the way I've learned to. There's no victory in that. There's no pride.

There's just the quiet determination to not let this take more from me than it already has. The familiar weight stays with me as the day unfolds. It doesn't dominate every moment, but it never fully leaves.

It sits there, reminding me that relapse doesn't erase what I've learned, but it does ask me to use it again, sooner than I wanted, on a day I didn't feel ready for. And that realization lingers, heavy and frustrating, as I keep going anyway, already aware that this is only the beginning of what this relapse will ask of me. The doubt doesn't rush in all at once. It slips in quietly, disguised as a reasonable question, the kind that sounds logical enough not to argue with at first. If this is back again, what did all that work actually remember? What stuck, and what just felt temporary? I hate how convincing that thought can be. It doesn't accuse me outright. It doesn't say I failed. It just wonders aloud whether I ever really moved forward at all. Whether the steadier days were real or just the absence of pressure.

Whether I was coping or simply distracted. The doubt sits there patiently, letting me fill in the worst conclusions on my own. I replay the past few months in my head. The rules I learned. The days I stayed. The small wins I allowed myself to count. And suddenly they feel fragile, like something that could disappear the moment things get heavy again. I don't want to believe that, but relapse has a way of shrinking your memory, of making it hard to trust anything that isn't happening right now. This is where it gets personal. I start questioning myself, not in a harsh way, but in a tired one. Was I actually doing better, or was I just managing better until this showed up again? Did I change, or did things just calm down long enough for me to think I had? Those questions don't come with answers. They just circle, feeding the sense that maybe none of this was as solid as I thought. There's grief in that realization. Grief for the steadier version of me I had started to trust. The one who believed they had learned how to live with this. The one who felt grounded enough to think maybe this time would be different. Feeling that trust wobble hurts more than the symptoms themselves. I don't feel panicked. I feel disappointed. Disappointed that I have to revisit this mental space again. Disappointed that the certainty I worked so hard to build feels thinner now.

Disappointed that progress doesn't protect me the way I secretly hoped it would. The worst part is how convincing relapse can sound. It tells me this is proof. Proof that this is just how it goes. Proof that no matter what I learn, this will always come back and demand attention. It frames itself as realism, as honesty, as something I should accept without question. I try not to engage with that voice too much. I've learned that arguing with it aggressively only gives it more space. Instead, I notice it. I acknowledge the doubt without letting it rewrite everything I know. That's harder than it sounds, especially when the heaviness is already pressing down and my energy is limited. I remind myself quietly that doubt doesn't mean erasure. The fact that this feels familiar doesn't mean I'm back at the beginning. The fact that it's hard again doesn't mean nothing changed. But believing that requires effort, and effort is in short supply on days like this. So I sit with the doubt. I don't resolve it. I don't defeat it. I let it exist alongside everything else I'm feeling, aware of how persuasive it can be without letting it become the only truth. That balancing act doesn't feel strong. It feels careful and deliberate. Like holding something fragile without knowing whether it will hold its shape. The doubt lingers as the day goes on, quiet but persistent, testing the steadiness I thought I had built. And even though it unsettles me, even though it makes everything feel less certain, I stay. Not confidently. Not convincingly. Just enough to keep going, knowing that questioning progress doesn't erase it, even when it feels unsteady in my hands.

The doubt eventually gives way to something heavier than sadness. Anger. Not explosive, not loud, just a steady irritation that sits in my chest and refuses to move. It isn't aimed at anyone in particular. It's aimed at the fact that I have to do this again. I don't feel broken. I feel worn down. There's a difference. I'm angry at the repetition. At the unfairness of knowing exactly what this takes and still having to pay the cost. Angry that awareness doesn't come with relief. Angry that I can do everything "right" and still wake up to the same weight pressing down on me. It feels like being handed a responsibility I never agreed to keep carrying. The exhaustion that follows is deep. Not the kind that sleep fixes. The kind that settles in because I know what's ahead of me. I know how many small decisions this will require. How much restraint. How much internal management just to keep things from tipping too far.

That knowledge alone drains me. I think about how tired I am of being responsible for my own mind. Of having to notice myself constantly. Of having to regulate, redirect, slow down, adjust. I don't want to be this aware today. I don't want to be careful. I don't want to manage myself. I want to move through a day without monitoring my internal state like it's something fragile.

That's where the anger sharpens. It's not dramatic. It's resentful. A quiet bitterness at the idea that this is part of my life now, whether I like it or not. I don't feel sorry for myself. I feel frustrated that no matter how much work I've done, this still shows up and asks more of me. I don't say any of this out loud. From the outside, I look the same. Inside, I'm negotiating with my own capacity, deciding how much I can give today without crossing a line I'll regret later. That negotiation never ends, and some days I hate that it exists at all. There's a moment where I consider withdrawing. Not disappearing entirely. Just pulling back enough to conserve energy. Doing the bare minimum. Shrinking my world down to something manageable. That instinct isn't weakness. It's self-protection. But it also comes with a cost, and I feel that tension clearly now. I don't want to lose ground. That's the part that surprises me. Even in the middle of frustration and fatigue, there's a quiet refusal to let this take more from me than it already has. I don't want to give up the steadiness I built, even if it feels thin right now. I don't want to disappear just because things are hard again. So I keep going, irritated and exhausted. Not motivated. Not hopeful. Just committed enough to not let anger make the decisions for me. That effort doesn't feel strong. It feels stubborn. It feels like choosing not to collapse even when collapsing would feel justified. The exhaustion stays with me as the day unfolds. It colors everything, slows me down, makes patience harder to find. But it doesn't erase what I've learned. It doesn't undo the fact that I'm still here, still aware, still capable of making choices even when I'm angry that I have to. Relapse doesn't make me fall apart. It makes me tired. Learning to carry that tiredness without turning it into self-blame becomes part of the work I didn't ask for but am still doing, one heavy step at a time.

By the end of the day, nothing is resolved. The heaviness hasn't lifted. The doubt hasn't fully quieted. The exhaustion still sits in my body like something earned but unwanted. There's no moment where I can point and say this is where it turned around. And yet, I'm still here. That realization doesn't arrive with relief. It arrives almost unnoticed, tucked into the ordinary act of the day ending. I didn't collapse. I didn't disappear. I didn't undo everything I'd learned just because this came back again. The relapse didn't take as much from me as it used to, even though it asked more than I wanted to give. I don't feel strong. I feel spent, but present. That matters more than I expect it to. In the past, a return like this would have swallowed me whole. It would have convinced me that nothing I did mattered, that all progress was an illusion. Now, even in the middle of frustration and doubt, there's a quiet awareness that I didn't lose myself entirely. I carried the weight and kept going. Not gracefully. Not confidently. But deliberately enough to stay engaged with my life instead of checking out of it. That doesn't erase the discomfort. It doesn't soften the truth that this may happen again. What it does is remind me that relapse isn't the same as erasure.

I didn't start over. I didn't fall back to the beginning. I moved through something familiar with more awareness than before, even if that awareness felt heavy and inconvenient. I noticed what was happening without turning it into a catastrophe. I allowed the day to be hard without letting it convince me that everything else was meaningless. That's new. Subtle. Easy to overlook. But real. I don't end this chapter feeling settled. I don't feel reassured about the future. There's still uncertainty, still fatigue, still the quiet fear that this could repeat itself in ways I'm not ready for. I don't pretend otherwise. What I do know is this: relapse didn't take me out. It tested the ground I've built and found it thinner than I wanted but not gone. I'm still standing on something, even if it feels unsteady. I'm still here inside my life, carrying the weight, moving forward without clarity, without certainty, without a clean ending. That has to count, not as a victory, not as proof of healing but as evidence. Evidence that even when it comes back, even when the heaviness returns and the doubt gets loud and the exhaustion settles deep, I don't disappear the way I once did. I don't lose everything

I've learned just because I'm tired. This chapter doesn't close with comfort. It closes with truth.

Relapse didn't undo me. It didn't define me. It didn't send me back to who I was at my worst. It reminded me that this isn't linear, that this isn't finished, that this is something I'll likely have to carry in different forms. And still, I stayed. Even now. Even like this. That steadiness, fragile as it feels, is enough to move forward into whatever comes next, knowing that relapse is not the end of the story — just another part of it.

Chapter 13

Rewriting Identity – Who am I now?

I miss the ambition I had before all of this. The way the future used to feel open instead of heavy. I miss having dreams that pulled me forward instead of questions that stopped me in my tracks. There was a version of me who moved through life with direction, who made plans without wondering whether my mind would cooperate long enough to see them through. Back then, I didn't question my ability to want things. I had goals. Not vague ones. Real ones. Things I worked toward with a sense of purpose that felt natural, almost automatic. I didn't need to talk myself into caring about the future. I didn't need to negotiate with my own energy or motivation. I assumed I would keep going, growing, building something that made sense. I trusted that. Losing that trust didn't happen overnight. It faded quietly, piece by piece, as anxiety and depression began reshaping how I experienced time.

The future stopped feeling like something I was moving toward and started feeling like something I had to brace for. Dreams didn't disappear, but they became harder to hold. Planning started to feel risky. Wanting too much felt dangerous. I didn't stop having ambition. It stopped feeling safe. I notice the difference now when I think about the life I imagined for myself. There's grief there, but it's complicated. I don't just miss the outcomes I wanted. I miss the version of me who believed in their ability to pursue them without constantly checking in on their own limits. I miss the ease of forward motion, the confidence that effort would lead somewhere meaningful. Now everything feels conditional. Dreams come with disclaimers. Goals come with caveats. I find myself asking quieter questions instead of making bold plans. Can I handle this? Will this cost me more than I can give? What happens if I get there and my mind doesn't let me enjoy it?

Those questions didn't used to exist. And realizing that hurts in a way that's hard to explain. It's not nostalgia. It's mourning. Mourning the loss of a version of myself who lived with momentum, who believed the future was something to build instead of something to survive. I don't hate who I am now. That's important. This isn't about wishing everything away or pretending the old me was perfect. I've learned things. I've gained awareness. I've built resilience I didn't know I was capable of. But I can still grieve what changed without wanting to undo
everything. The ambition I miss wasn't just about success. It was about possibility. About waking up and feeling pulled toward something instead of weighed down by what might go wrong. About trusting that my mind would support me instead of working against me. About believing that effort was worth it because the future felt reachable. Now the future feels quieter. Smaller. Closer to the present moment. And while that has taught me how to survive, it's also taken something from me. Something I didn't realize I valued until it was gone. I carry that loss with me as I try to understand who I am now, knowing that I'm no longer the person who chased life with the same certainty, but not yet sure who I'm becoming instead. That uncertainty sits with me, not as panic, and not as despair. As a quiet ache for the life I once

imagined, and the person I was when imagining it didn't require so much courage.

For a long time, I knew who I was because I could describe myself easily. My goals explained me. My drive gave me shape. I understood myself through what I was building and where I was headed. That clarity made decisions feel simple, even when life wasn't. Now that language doesn't come as easily. When I try to describe who I am now, I hesitate. Not because I don't exist, but because the labels I used to rely on don't fit the way they used to. Ambitious. Driven. Future-focused. Those words feel incomplete now, like they belong to someone I remember rather than someone I fully recognize. I'm still me. That's the strange part. I haven't disappeared. My values didn't vanish. I still care deeply. I still want things. But the way I move through the world has changed enough that the old definitions don't hold the same weight. I don't know how to summarize myself anymore, and that uncertainty feels unsettling. There's comfort in labels, even when they're limiting. They give you a way to explain yourself quickly, a way to be understood without having to unpack everything. Losing that feels like losing a map. I move through life now without a clear sense of how to introduce myself, even to myself.

Who am I, if not the person I was becoming? That question doesn't demand an answer right away. It just lingers. I notice it when I make decisions, when I think about the future, when I compare myself to people who seem to move with more certainty than I do. I'm no longer chasing an identity. I'm navigating without one. That feels uncomfortable. There's a temptation to rush toward a new label, to replace what I lost with something that makes sense again. Survivor. Resilient. Healing. Strong. Those words are available, but they don't feel quite right either. They explain my experience, not my identity. I don't want to reduce myself to what I've been through. At the same time, I can't pretend it didn't change me.

Living with anxiety and depression reshaped how I see the world, how I prioritize, how I measure success. Ignoring that would feel dishonest. Letting it define me completely would feel suffocating. So I sit in between. Between who I was and who I'm not yet. Between ambition and caution. Between wanting and protecting myself. Living without a clear label feels disorienting, but it also feels honest. I'm no longer forcing myself into a description that doesn't fit just to feel understood. There's grief in that honesty. I miss the simplicity of knowing exactly how to describe myself. I miss the confidence that came with having a clear direction. But there's also a strange relief in not having to perform an identity I'm no longer aligned with.

I don't have to explain myself as much now. I don't have to meet expectations tied to a version of me that doesn't exist anymore. That freedom doesn't feel empowering yet. It feels quiet. Uncertain. Still taking shape. Living without a label forces me to pay attention to who I am in practice rather than in theory. How I treat myself. How I move through difficulty. What I protect. What I let go of. Those things don't fit neatly into a title, but they feel more real than the labels I used to rely on. I don't know who I am now in a way I can summarize. But I'm learning that not knowing doesn't mean I'm lost. It means I'm in the middle of something unfinished, something still forming, something that doesn't need a name yet to be valid.

Some of the biggest changes happened without my permission. I didn't wake up one day and decide to become more cautious, more inward, more protective of my energy. It happened slowly, in response to what I needed to survive, not what I wanted to become. Looking back, I can see how my priorities shifted long before I consciously acknowledged them. I care differently now. Not less — differently. I notice what drains me faster. I notice what feels heavy even when it looks harmless. I don't push myself into situations just because I should be able to handle them. I don't chase urgency the way I used to.

What once felt exciting now sometimes feels overwhelming, and that realization still catches me off guard. I've become more selective. With my time. With my energy. With the parts of myself I offer to the world. Before, I gave freely without thinking about the cost. Now I calculate, not because I'm selfish, but because I've learned what it feels like to run out completely. That awareness didn't come from wisdom. It came from necessity. My definition of success changed too. It used to mean forward motion, achievement, building something visible. Now it's quieter. It's sustainability. It's being able to keep showing up without losing myself in the process. I don't measure my worth by how much I produce anymore. I measure it by how intact I can stay while living my life. That shift feels both grounding and unsettling. Grounding, because it protects me.

Unsettling, because it distances me from the person I thought I was supposed to be. I notice how my relationships have changed as well. I'm less performative. Less eager to prove I'm okay. I don't fill silence as quickly. I don't force myself to be upbeat when I'm not. That honesty costs me sometimes. It makes some people uncomfortable. It changes dynamics in ways I didn't anticipate. I didn't plan for that. I didn't plan to become someone who values depth over momentum, steadiness over ambition, presence over potential. Those values emerged because they had to. Because the version of me who chased constantly didn't survive what came next. There's grief in realizing this. Not because these changes are bad, but because they mark a clear distance between who I was and who I am now. I can't go back to caring the way I used to, even if I wanted to. I've seen too much of what ignoring myself costs. And yet, there's something honest about this version of me. I don't live on autopilot anymore.

I don't assume I'm invincible. I don't treat my mind like something I can override indefinitely. Those changes don't feel empowering. They feel sobering. They ask me to live more intentionally, even when I miss the ease of moving without thinking. I didn't choose these changes. But they're real. And acknowledging them helps me understand why the old identity doesn't fit anymore. Why trying to return to it feels impossible. The person I was before didn't need these boundaries. The person I am now does. That doesn't mean I'm weaker. It means I'm different. And sitting with that difference, without rushing to label it or justify it, becomes part of rewriting who I am — not by force, but by noticing what has quietly reshaped me along the way. The grief doesn't show up as regret. I don't sit around wishing I could undo everything or pretending that going back would fix this. I know too much now. I've lived too deeply inside this version of myself to believe that returning is possible, or even desirable in the way nostalgia tries to sell it. Still, the grief is real. I grieve the version of me who didn't have to think this hard just to exist. The one who made plans without calculating the emotional cost.

The one who could dream without immediately wondering what it would take to survive the process of chasing those dreams. That version of me didn't know how fragile things could feel, and I miss that innocence more than I miss the outcomes themselves. I don't want my old life back. I want the ease that came with it. That distinction matters. I'm not romanticizing the past or pretending it was perfect. I'm mourning the loss of effortlessness, the way life used to move without so much internal resistance. The way ambition felt energizing instead of risky. The way the future felt like an invitation instead of a question mark. This grief is quiet. It shows up in small moments, when I catch myself hesitating before committing to something that once would have excited me. When I feel a pang of sadness watching other people move forward without the same internal negotiations. When I realize that even on good days, there's a layer of caution that never fully leaves. I don't resent who I've become.

That surprises me. I expected grief to come with bitterness or anger or a desire to reject this version of myself. Instead, it comes with tenderness. A soft acknowledgment that something meaningful was lost, even if what replaced it was necessary. I can hold both truths at once. I can accept that I've changed in ways that keep me alive. And I can mourn the parts of me that didn't make it through unchanged. Those feelings don't cancel each other out. They coexist, sometimes uncomfortably, sometimes quietly, always honestly. I don't need to choose between honoring who I was and respecting who I am now. There are moments when the grief catches me off guard. It doesn't announce itself. It slips in during ordinary thoughts, when I remember how certain I once felt about where I was going, how confident I was in my ability to get there. That certainty didn't survive this. And even though I understand why, even though I know I couldn't carry it forward unchanged, losing it still hurts. I let that hurt exist without trying to resolve it. I don't tell myself everything happens for a reason. I don't frame the loss as necessary growth. I don't rush toward gratitude. I let the grief be what it is — an acknowledgment that something mattered, and that its absence leaves a mark. Grieving without wanting to go back feels strange. It's not longing, It's recognition.

Recognition that my identity isn't something I traded willingly. It was reshaped by experience, by survival, by learning how to live in a body and mind that demanded different things. I didn't choose to lose parts of myself, but I can choose to honor them without letting them define me entirely. This grief doesn't ask me to undo anything. It just asks me to be honest about what changed, about what I miss, about what can't be carried forward the same way. And sitting with that honesty, even when it feels heavy, brings a quiet kind of clarity. I'm not trying to become who I was again. I'm learning how to live with the truth that I'm not them anymore, while still respecting what they gave me, what they believed in, and what they hoped for before everything shifted. At some point, I stop trying to replace what I lost with something equally clear. I stop searching for a new version of myself that I can explain easily or commit to confidently. The need for definition loosens, not because I've figured anything out, but because forcing an identity no longer feels honest. I don't know who I'm becoming. That used to terrify me. I wanted answers. Direction. A sense of arrival. I wanted to feel anchored to something solid the way I used to be anchored to ambition and plans. Letting go of that certainty felt like drifting at first, like existing without a shape. Now it feels different. It feels like space. Space to live without constant self-evaluation.

Space to exist without needing to justify my pace or my priorities. Space to be present without measuring myself against a version of life that no longer fits. I'm not replacing my old identity with a new one. I'm allowing myself to be undefined for now. That doesn't mean I'm empty. It means I'm paying attention. I notice who I am in moments rather than who I am in theory. I notice how I show up when things are hard. I notice what I protect instinctively. I notice what I no longer tolerate. Those things tell me more about who I am now than any label ever could. There's a quiet relief in not having to know. I don't need to introduce myself to my own future yet. I don't need to promise anything or prove anything or build a narrative that makes sense to other people. I just need to stay present in my life as it is, letting identity emerge instead of demanding it arrive fully formed. This way of being feels less impressive. But it feels more honest. I don't have the ambition I once had, not in the same way, not with the same urgency.

What I have instead is an awareness of what matters enough to protect. A sense of limits I didn't used to respect. A willingness to move slowly if it means staying intact. That's not the story I expected to tell about myself. But it's the one I'm living. Becoming undefined doesn't mean giving up on the future. It means loosening my grip on what I thought it had to look like. It means allowing room for change without demanding that it follow a specific timeline or lead to a specific outcome. I'm still here. Not fully formed. Not clearly labeled. But present, aware, and engaged in my life in a way that doesn't require certainty to feel real. That has to be enough for now. This chapter doesn't end with clarity. It ends with permission. Permission to exist without knowing who I am becoming yet. Permission to let identity be fluid instead of fixed. Permission to honor who I was without forcing myself to return to them. I don't have a new definition for myself. I have space. And in that space, something quieter, steadier, and more sustainable is taking shape, even if I can't name it yet.

Chapter 14

Building Tools – Coping skills that actually help

For a long time, I was told to stay positive. As if positivity was something I could reach for if I just tried harder. As if the problem wasn't that I couldn't see anything good, but that I wasn't looking in the right direction. I tried. I really did. I repeated the words. I nodded along. I told myself things would get better even when I didn't believe it. Inside, it felt hollow. Positivity didn't land as hope. It landed as pressure. Pressure to feel something I couldn't access. Pressure to pretend life still felt meaningful when it didn't. The more I tried to stay positive, the more disconnected I felt from myself, like I was betraying my own reality just to appear okay. Pushing through was supposed to be strength. That was the other thing people leaned on. Keep going. Don't stop. Push through it. As if momentum alone could carry me somewhere better. But there were days when nothing mattered enough to push toward. Days when effort felt pointless because the future didn't feel real. Pushing through didn't make me stronger. It made me resentful. It drained what little energy I had left. There's a difference between endurance and erasure.

Pushing through asked me to ignore how bad things felt. Staying positive asked me to deny it altogether. Neither helped. Both made me feel like I was failing at something I was never equipped to do in the first place. I wasn't struggling because I lacked motivation or optimism. I was struggling because my internal world had gone quiet in a way that words like "hope" couldn't reach. I remember thinking that if this was the answer, then something must be wrong with me. Why couldn't I just reframe things? Why didn't gratitude shift anything? Why did forcing myself forward only make the emptiness louder? It took a long time to understand that the advice wasn't wrong because it was useless — it was wrong because it didn't match what I was living. You can't stay positive when you don't feel connected to life.

You can't push through when the ground you're standing on doesn't feel solid enough to push off from. Those ideas assume there's something to build on. There wasn't. Not yet. Letting go of those expectations felt like failure at first. Like I was admitting defeat. Like I was giving up on improvement. But what I was actually doing was stopping the damage. I was allowing myself to tell the truth instead of forcing a version of myself that sounded healthier than it felt. That was the first real shift. Not learning what *to* do — but admitting what didn't help. Admitting that pretending, reframing, and forcing movement weren't tools for me. They were masks. And masks take energy I didn't have. I didn't need positivity. I needed honesty. I didn't need to push. I needed something that wouldn't make things worse.

Recognizing what didn't work wasn't a breakthrough. It was a quiet clearing. Making room for something more realistic. Something less impressive. Something that didn't require me to believe in a future I couldn't feel yet. This chapter doesn't start with solutions. It starts with subtraction. With letting go of the advice that sounded good but didn't keep me here. With acknowledging that staying alive required something different than optimism and grit. Something smaller. Something steadier. Something that didn't ask me to lie to myself.

I didn't learn my warning signs because I wanted to. I learned them because ignoring them cost me more than I could afford to lose. At first, everything felt like it happened all at once. One moment I was fine, the next I wasn't. There didn't seem to be a pattern, just sudden drops that left me scrambling to catch up. Over time, I realized there were signals. I just wasn't listening yet. They weren't dramatic. There was no clear alarm going off. It was subtler than that. A shift in my patience. A heaviness that showed up earlier in the day than usual. The way my thoughts started looping instead of moving forward. The urge to withdraw before anything was actually wrong. Those were the signs. I used to ignore them because they didn't feel serious enough. I told myself I was overthinking. That everyone gets tired. That pushing through was still the responsible thing to do. By the time I admitted something was off, I was already too deep in it to respond gently. Learning my signals meant slowing down enough to notice the early changes. Not to fix them. Not to analyze them. Just to acknowledge them without judgment. That took practice. It also took a lot of missteps. I didn't suddenly become self-aware in a graceful way.

I noticed patterns because I repeated them enough times to recognize the cost. Each time I pushed past my limits, the aftermath was harder to recover from. Each time I ignored the signs, the fallout lasted longer. Eventually, I stopped asking whether I was allowed to take them seriously. I stopped waiting for things to get bad enough to justify slowing down. I learned that the earlier signs mattered more than the later ones. That prevention didn't look like control. It looked like listening. Some days, the signal is emotional. A flatness that creeps in quietly. A lack of interest in things I normally tolerate. Irritability that doesn't match the situation. Other days, it's physical. Tension that doesn't release. Fatigue that feels disproportionate. A sense of heaviness that settles in before I've done anything to earn it. I don't treat these signs as emergencies. I treat them as information. They don't mean I'm failing. They don't mean something terrible is about to happen. They mean I need to adjust before the adjustment is forced on me. That shift in perspective took time. I had to stop seeing self-awareness as indulgence and start seeing it as maintenance.

Listening doesn't always change how I feel. Sometimes the heaviness stays. Sometimes the anxiety hums anyway. But acknowledging the signals gives me options. It lets me respond instead of reacting. It creates space between the first sign of trouble and the full spiral that used to follow. That space matters. It's the difference between a hard day and a crash. Between discomfort and collapse. Between needing to recover and needing to rebuild. I don't always get it right, but more often now, I notice sooner. Learning my signals didn't make life easier. It made it more manageable. And that, for me, is what a real tool looks like. Not something that fixes the problem, but something that reduces the damage. Something that keeps me here long enough to get through another day without losing more ground than necessary.

The things that help me most aren't impressive. They don't feel transformative or empowering. They don't give me a sense of accomplishment. Most of the time, they feel almost disappointing in how small they are. But they work in the only way that matters to me now — they keep things from getting worse.I stopped looking for tools that would make me feel better. I started looking for tools that would help me *not fall apart.* That shift changed everything. Some days, the most useful thing I can do is narrow my world. Not in a dramatic way, not isolating completely, just shrinking the radius of what I expect from myself. Fewer decisions. Fewer commitments. Less input. When my mind is loud or heavy, simplicity becomes protection. Structure helps more than motivation ever did. Having a loose routine gives my day shape when my internal world feels chaotic. I don't rely on feeling ready or inspired. I rely on familiarity. Doing the same few things in roughly the same order gives me something steady to move through when my thoughts aren't cooperative. Distraction is another tool I had to stop judging. For a long time, I told myself distraction meant avoidance, that if I wasn't fully processing everything all the time, I was doing something wrong. Now I understand that intentional distraction can be regulation. Letting my attention rest somewhere neutral can give my nervous system a break without pretending nothing is wrong. Rest becomes preventative. Not something I earn after surviving the day, but something I use to keep the day survivable. I stop waiting until I'm depleted to slow down. I try to pause earlier, even when part of me insists I should keep pushing. That pause doesn't always feel good. It feels cautious. But it keeps me from crossing lines that take longer to recover from.

Lowering expectations is a tool too. Not in a giving-up way. In a realistic one. I stop measuring my days by what I should be able to do and start measuring them by what I can actually manage. Some days that's more. Some days it's less. Letting that fluctuate without turning it into a judgment helps more than forcing consistency ever did. None of these tools feel like solutions. They don't change how my mind works. They don't make the heaviness disappear. They don't stop relapse from happening. What they do is soften the impact. They keep a hard day from becoming a breaking point. They give me enough stability to stay present instead of shutting down completely. That's all I ask of them. I don't need tools that fix me. I need tools that keep me intact. Most of the time, using them feels unremarkable. Sometimes it even feels like settling. But I've learned that survival doesn't need to feel inspiring to be effective. It just needs to work well enough to get me through the day without taking more from me than necessary. These tools don't look like progress from the outside. They look like maintenance. Quiet, repetitive, often invisible maintenance that keeps things running even when nothing feels good. And I've come to respect that kind of work more than anything flashy or dramatic. Because it keeps me here. Learning what helps is only part of it.

The harder part is letting myself use those tools without judging myself for needing them. There's a voice that still shows up sometimes, quietly questioning whether this is really living or just managing, whether relying on structure and rest and distraction means I've lowered the bar too far. That voice sounds convincing. It tells me I should be stronger by now. That if I've learned so much, I shouldn't need these accommodations. That needing tool means something is still wrong. I used to listen to that voice and push past what helped, just to prove I could. Every time I did that, I paid for it later. Shame made everything worse. It turned simple coping into a moral issue. Rest became laziness. Distraction became avoidance. Lowering expectations became failure. I wasn't just struggling — I was criticizing myself for struggling, and that second layer of pressure was often heavier than the anxiety or depression themselves. It took time to unlearn that. I had to stop treating survival strategies like evidence against me.

I had to remind myself that needing support doesn't mean I'm weak, and using tools doesn't mean I'm broken. It means I'm responding honestly to the reality of my life as it is now, not as I wish it were. There are days when I still feel embarrassed by how small my world needs to be. Days when I compare myself to people who seem to do more, carry more, push further without consequence. That comparison creeps in quietly, making my tools feel inadequate or childish or unnecessary. On those days, it takes effort to stay grounded in what I know actually works for me. What works isn't always impressive. Sometimes it's choosing a familiar routine instead of trying something new. Sometimes it's letting myself disengage early instead of forcing presence. Sometimes it's doing less and calling that enough. None of that fits neatly into a story about growth or resilience. But it keeps me here. Using tools without shame means letting go of the idea that coping should look a certain way. It means accepting that my nervous system has limits, and respecting those limits isn't a failure of character. It's a form of care I didn't know how to offer myself before. I stop asking whether I *should* need these tools. I start asking whether they help me stay intact. That shift feels subtle, but it changes everything. It takes the pressure off performing wellness and puts the focus back on staying present in my life without doing unnecessary harm to myself. Some days, I still resist.

Some days, I want to believe I don't need the extra support anymore. When I push through anyway, the result is almost always the same — more fatigue, more heaviness, more recovery time. Those days remind me that shame doesn't make me stronger. It just makes the work harder. Letting go of shame doesn't make the tools feel good. It makes them usable. And that matters more than pride. It matters more than appearances. It matters more than living up to an idea of strength that doesn't match my reality anymore. I don't need to justify how I cope. I need to keep myself here. And learning to use the tools that help me do that, without turning them into evidence of failure, becomes its own form of progress — quiet, uncelebrated, but deeply necessary. At some point, I stop calling this healing. Not because nothing has changed, but because that word comes with expectations I can't live up to. Healing suggests an endpoint.

A moment where things settle, where the work is done, where the tools are no longer necessary. That hasn't been my experience. What I'm doing is maintenance. Daily. Ongoing. Unremarkable maintenance. The kind you don't notice when it's working and only feel when you stop doing it. It doesn't feel like progress in the way people talk about progress. It feels like keeping things from falling apart again. That used to disappoint me. I wanted to believe all this effort would lead somewhere cleaner, somewhere lighter. I wanted proof that I was getting better in a way that meant I wouldn't have to keep watching myself so closely. Accepting that this might be ongoing felt like giving something up. Now it feels like telling the truth.

Maintenance doesn't mean I've failed to heal. It means I've learned what my life requires to stay livable. It means I understand my limits well enough to work with them instead of pretending they don't exist. It means I've stopped chasing a version of myself that doesn't need support. Some days, maintenance feels manageable. Other days, it feels tedious. Like I'm stuck doing the same internal tasks over and over again without visible reward. Those days test my patience. They make me wonder how long I'll have to keep doing this, how many times I'll have to notice the same signs, make the same adjustments, protect the same boundaries. I don't have an answer to that. What I have is experience. Experience has taught me that when I stop maintaining, things deteriorate quietly at first, then all at once. When I stay consistent, even imperfectly, life remains something I can move through without losing myself completely. That's enough for now. I don't frame this as acceptance in a polished way. I don't say I'm at peace with it. I say I understand it. I understand that my mind and body require ongoing care, not because they're broken, but because they've been through something that changed how they function.

Maintenance doesn't make me feel hopeful. It makes me feel grounded. Grounded in the reality of my life as it is, not as I wish it would be. Grounded in the knowledge that I can keep going without demanding transformation from myself. Grounded in the fact that staying present takes work, and that work deserves respect, not dismissal. This chapter doesn't end with solutions. It ends with permission. Permission to use what helps without shame. Permission to call maintenance enough. Permission to stop waiting for a finish line before valuing the effort it takes to stay here. I don't need to be healed to keep living.

I just need to keep maintaining what allows me to exist without losing more ground than necessary. And learning to honor that work, even when it feels repetitive and unspectacular, is one of the most important things I've done. Not because it fixes everything. Because it keeps me here.

Chapter 15

Hope, Slowly – What healing really looks like

I didn't notice hope arriving at first. It didn't come with a feeling or a realization or a shift I could name. It showed up quietly, disguised as something smaller. One morning, I woke up and didn't dread the day ahead of me. Not because I felt good, not because I was excited — but because the weight wasn't there in the same way. I didn't immediately recognize that as anything important. It felt neutral. Ordinary. Just a morning where my first thought wasn't resistance. I didn't have to talk myself into getting out of bed. I didn't lie there bargaining with the day, already exhausted by the idea of moving through it. I noticed the absence before I noticed the meaning. I wasn't dreading waking up. That alone felt unfamiliar. For so long, mornings had carried their own heaviness. Not panic, not despair — just a deep reluctance to start again. The effort it took to face another day, another stretch of time, another cycle of managing myself had been overwhelming. Waking up used to feel like being asked to carry something I didn't have the energy for yet. This time, that resistance wasn't there.

It didn't mean I felt motivated. It didn't mean I wanted the day. It just meant I wasn't actively pushing against it. I could exist in the morning without bracing myself. That felt small enough to overlook, but different enough to stay with me. Going to work felt the same way. I didn't suddenly enjoy it again. I didn't feel fulfilled or driven or engaged. I just didn't dread the act of going. The thought of pushing myself through the day didn't feel unbearable. It felt manageable. Neutral. Possible. That was new. I didn't label it as hope right away. Hope felt like too big a word for something this quiet. This didn't feel like belief or optimism or trust in the future. It felt like the absence of resistance. Like the space where dread used to sit had opened just enough for me to move. I didn't try to hold onto it. I didn't analyze it or question it or wonder how long it would last. I let it exist without assigning meaning, because assigning meaning felt like pressure. I didn't want to scare it away by expecting too much from it. Still, I noticed. I noticed how different the day felt when I wasn't fighting it from the start. How much energy that freed up.

How the absence of dread didn't make things good, but it made them lighter. Easier to step into without feeling like I was forcing myself through something impossible. That's how hope showed up for me. Not as a feeling, but as a reduction. Not as excitement, but as relief I didn't ask for. It didn't promise anything. It didn't say this would last. It just showed me that mornings didn't have to hurt the same way every time. And that was enough to notice. I didn't feel healed. I didn't feel fixed. But I felt less opposed to being here. And that small shift — waking up without dread, moving toward the day without resistance — felt like the earliest form of hope I could trust. Not because it asked me to believe in anything, but because it didn't ask me to fight anymore.

Letting the future back in didn't feel brave. It felt cautious, almost reluctant, like opening a door just enough to see what was on the other side without committing to step through it. For a long time, thinking ahead felt dangerous. The future carried too much pressure, too many unknowns, too many opportunities for disappointment. It was easier to keep my focus narrow, to live inside today and not ask anything more of myself. So when the future started to reappear in my thoughts, it caught me off guard. Not in big ways. I didn't start planning years ahead or dreaming out loud about what my life might look like. It was smaller than that. I noticed myself thinking about the next day without immediately shutting it down. Wondering about next week without feeling overwhelmed. Letting my mind drift just a little further forward than I used to. That was new. Before, those thoughts would trigger resistance. A tightening in my chest. A reflex to pull back. The idea of committing to anything beyond the present felt like setting myself up for failure. Now, the fear didn't disappear, but it softened. It gave me a little room to look ahead without panicking. I didn't trust it right away. I was careful not to mistake this for confidence. I didn't want to over-interpret what was happening or rush myself into expectations I couldn't meet. So, I kept the future small. Manageable. Close enough to touch without being forced to hold onto it. Sometimes it was as simple as thinking, I'll do that tomorrow. And not feeling dread immediately afterward. Other times, it was imagining myself still working, still showing up, still moving through life in ordinary ways weeks from now.

Those thoughts didn't feel hopeful. They felt tolerable. And that tolerance mattered more than belief ever did. Allowing the future back in didn't mean I trusted it. It meant I stopped rejecting it outright. There's a difference between believing things will be okay and allowing the possibility that they might not always be unbearable. I wasn't ready for belief. I wasn't ready for optimism. I was only ready to stop closing the door completely. That restraint felt protective. I didn't promise myself anything. I didn't say this meant things were improving or that the hard days were behind me. I just noticed that the future didn't feel as hostile as it once did. It didn't feel like something I had to defend myself against constantly. That shift didn't erase my anxiety. It didn't remove the heaviness or the uncertainty.

It just changed how much power those feelings had over my willingness to keep going. I could imagine myself continuing without immediately questioning whether I could handle it. That was enough. Letting the future back in slowly didn't feel like progress in the traditional sense. It felt like easing tension I'd been holding for a long time. Like releasing a grip, I didn't realize was exhausting me. I didn't lean into the future. I simply stopped pushing it away. And that subtle change made room for something gentler than hope. Not belief. Not certainty. Just the quiet permission to keep moving forward without assuming it would hurt the same way every time.

I used to think healing would feel obvious. Like something I would recognize immediately. Lighter. Clearer. Like a weightlifting in a way that made sense. When that didn't happen, I assumed it meant I wasn't healing at all, that I was just learning how to tolerate life instead of actually getting better. Now I understand how narrow that definition was. Healing didn't arrive as relief. It arrived as neutrality. As days that didn't hurt as sharply. As moments where my mind didn't immediately reach for the worst-case scenario. As the absence of constant resistance. None of that felt good enough to call progress at first. It felt almost disappointing, like I was settling for less than I deserved. But settling wasn't what was happening. I wasn't learning how to accept less from life. I was learning how to live without needing my internal experience to validate every step I took. Healing wasn't showing up as a rush of hope or a return of joy. It was showing up as stability I could lean on even when nothing felt particularly good. That took time to trust.

There were days when I wondered if this was as good as it was going to get. Days when I missed the idea of healing more than I missed the pain itself. The idea that one day I would wake up and know I was better had been comforting. Letting go of that expectation felt like another loss. But then I started noticing what was actually different. I wasn't fighting every moment anymore. I wasn't waking up already exhausted by the thought of existing. I wasn't constantly bracing for collapse. Those changes didn't feel celebratory. They felt quiet. Almost easy to miss if I wasn't paying attention. Healing, for me, wasn't a feeling. It was capacity. The ability to carry a little more without breaking. The ability to sit with discomfort without immediately trying to escape it. The ability to move through a day without narrating every thought as a threat. None of that came with a sense of accomplishment. It just showed up as something I could do now that I couldn't before. I stopped waiting to feel healed. I stopped using my emotions as proof that something was working. Emotions still fluctuate. Anxiety still hums.

Depression still dulls things from time to time. But underneath that, there's more room. More tolerance. More steadiness than there used to be. That steadiness doesn't announce itself. It doesn't feel like growth.

It doesn't feel like success. It feels like being able to stay in my life without constantly needing to escape it. And that realization changed how I measure healing entirely. Healing isn't about how I feel on my best days. It's about how I handle my worst ones. It's about how much space exists between a hard moment and a spiral. It's about how often I can choose to stay instead of shutting down completely. That kind of healing is easy to overlook. It doesn't give you stories to tell or milestones to celebrate. It just quietly changes what you're capable of enduring without losing yourself. And learning to recognize that, even when it doesn't come with emotional payoff, helps me trust that something real is happening here. Not dramatic. Not obvious. But real enough to keep going.

Trust didn't come back the way I expected it to. It didn't arrive as confidence or reassurance or a sense that things would work out. I didn't suddenly believe in life again. What returned was quieter than that, almost unnoticeable if I wasn't paying attention. I stopped if everything ahead of me would hurt. That was it. For a long time, life felt hostile by default. Every day was something to brace for, something to endure rather than enter. Even neutral moments felt suspicious, like they were only calm because something worse was waiting. Trust couldn't exist in that environment. There was nothing to place it on. Now, that assumption loosens slightly. I don't wake up believing the day will be good. I just don't automatically believe it will be unbearable. That difference might seem small, but it changes how I move through the hours. I don't grip the day as tightly. I don't watch myself constantly for signs that I'm about to fall apart. Trust, for me, becomes tolerance. Tolerance for uncertainty. Tolerance for discomfort. Tolerance for the idea that I can continue without knowing how things will unfold. I don't need guarantees anymore. I just need the absence of immediate threat, and most days, that's enough to keep me moving. I'm careful with this. I don't rush into belief. I don't make promises to myself about the future. I don't frame this as faith or optimism.

I let trust exist as a quiet willingness to participate without needing proof that it will be worth it. There are still moments when the old fear resurfaces. Moments when my mind jumps ahead and starts asking the familiar questions. What if this doesn't last? What if I lose this steadiness? What if things get worse again? Those thoughts haven't disappeared. They just don't control me the way they used to. I don't argue with them anymore. I let them exist without turning them into decisions. I don't need to convince myself that everything will be okay. I just need to tolerate not knowing.

That tolerance feels like the most honest form of trust I've been capable of. Trusting life carefully means staying open without expectation. It means letting moments happen without immediately measuring them. It means allowing myself to exist in the present without constantly preparing for the next collapse. That doesn't mean I feel safe all the time. It means I feel less guarded. That's new. I notice how that careful trust changes my relationship with myself. I don't scrutinize every good moment as if it needs defending. I don't punish myself for feeling okay. I let neutral and steady days exist without suspicion. Trust doesn't feel warm. It feels calm, reserved, and deliberate. And that's exactly what I need it to be. I don't need life to promise me anything. I just need it to stop feeling like something I have to survive at all costs. Learning to trust it carefully, without belief or certainty, gives me just enough room to keep showing up without fear leading every step.

I don't end this chapter with certainty. I don't have a conclusion that ties everything together or a belief that carries me forward without effort. What I have instead is a willingness to stay open, even when I don't know what that openness will ask of me. For a long time, staying open felt dangerous. It meant risking disappointment. It meant allowing myself to want things again. It meant letting the future exist without shutting it down preemptively. Closing myself off felt safer, more controlled, like a way to protect myself from hope becoming another thing I'd lose. Now, I see how much that closure cost me. Staying open doesn't mean I expect good things to happen. It doesn't mean I trust that life will be kind or easy or fair. It means I'm no longer refusing the possibility of continuation. I'm no longer bracing myself against every moment as if it's something I have to survive rather than live through. That openness is fragile. Some days it's barely there. Some days it closes again without warning. I don't force it to stay. I don't shame myself when it disappears. I understand now that openness, like everything else, comes and goes. What matters is that it's possible at all. I let myself imagine small things without immediately dismissing them.

A day that goes smoothly. A week that feels manageable. A future version of myself still here, still working, still navigating life with the tools I've built. Those thoughts don't feel hopeful. They feel allowable. And that allowance changes how I experience the present. I don't need hope to be loud. I don't need it to motivate me or inspire me or reassure me. I just need it to exist quietly in the background, like permission to keep going without knowing where I'm headed. Hope, for me, has become less about believing in outcomes and more about not closing myself off from the possibility of living. Staying open doesn't fix anything. It doesn't guarantee that hard days won't return. It doesn't promise that anxiety or depression won't flare up again. What it does is keep me from hardening against my own life. It keeps me from deciding too early that nothing is worth engaging with. That feels important. I don't owe myself optimism. I don't owe myself belief.

I owe myself honesty and space. Space to exist without demanding certainty. Space to move forward without forcing meaning. Space to let life continue unfolding, even if I don't understand where it's going or how I'll feel along the way. This is what hope looks like for me now. Not a destination. Not a feeling. An openness I return to when I can, and release when I can't, knowing that the fact I can access it at all means something has shifted. I don't end here feeling resolved. I end here willing. Willing to stay. Willing to remain open.

Willing to let life keep happening without needing to know what it will become. And for now, that is enough to carry forward into whatever comes next.

Chapter 16

Living, Not Just Surviving – A new definition of life

Living, for me now, starts with something simple: I'm still alive, and I still have a life. Not the one I imagined before, not untouched by anxiety or depression, but a real one that continues to move forward whether I feel ready or not. For a long time, staying alive felt like the entire task. Every day was measured by how hard it was to get through it. Everything else faded into the background. Survival wasn't a phase — it was the focus. I didn't think about living. I thought about enduring. About getting through the hours without losing myself completely. Now, something has shifted. Not suddenly. Not cleanly. But enough that survival isn't the only thing defining my days anymore. I'm here inside my life again. I show up. I participate.

I move through the world knowing anxiety and depression are still present but no longer letting them be the final authority on how I live. This doesn't feel victorious. It feels grounded. I don't wake up thinking I've won anything. I wake up knowing I have a day in front of me, and that life doesn't stop just because my mind is loud sometimes. I've learned that this is simply a new way of living — not a temporary workaround, not a failure to recover, just a different relationship with myself and the world. Anxiety and depression didn't disappear. They still exist. They still show up. They still affect how I feel and how I move through things. But they don't get to decide whether my life continues.

They don't get to pause everything indefinitely. They don't get to define the entire meaning of my existence. Life goes on. And instead of fighting that reality or resenting it, I've learned how to live inside it. To adjust. To participate without waiting to feel perfect or healed or certain. To accept that this isn't about winning or losing — it's about continuing. Being here now feels different than surviving. There's more awareness. More presence. More texture to the days. I notice things again. I engage with moments instead of just bracing myself against them. I don't rush through time the way I used to, desperate to get to the end of the day. Living doesn't mean the absence of struggle. It means struggle isn't the only thing happening. I'm alive.

I have a life. Learning all of this hasn't been about defeating anxiety or depression. It's been about refusing to let them take everything. Refusing to let them be the reason life stops. Life must go on. Not in a forced way. Not in a motivational way. In a real, grounded, human way — one day at a time, with everything I carry, choosing to stay engaged in a life that's imperfect, ongoing, and still mine. The noise never left. Anxiety and depression didn't pack up and disappear once I learned how to live again. They're still here, still present in the background of my days, still capable of getting loud when I'm tired or overwhelmed or caught off guard. The difference now is that they no longer fill the entire room. I used to experience life *through* the noise. Everything passed through it first. Every thought, every decision, every moment was filtered through anxiety or weighed down by depression. It was impossible to separate what was real from what was internal. The noise wasn't just part of my life — it *was* my life. Now, it shares space. Some days it's louder. Other days it fades into the background enough that I can focus on what's in front of me. I don't measure my days by how quiet my mind is anymore. I measure them by whether I'm present despite the noise.

That shift matters. I no longer wait for silence before engaging with life. I don't postpone living until I feel calm or motivated or emotionally steady. If I did, I'd be waiting forever. Instead, I move forward knowing the noise may come with me, knowing it may interrupt, knowing it may try to take center stage again. And I let life happen anyway. This doesn't feel brave. It feels practical. I've learned that the noise feeds on resistance. The more I fight it, the more it demands attention. When I let it exist without letting it dominate, it loses some of its power. Not because it's gone — but because it's no longer the only thing I'm listening to. I notice the world more now. Small details. Familiar routines.

The rhythm of ordinary days. Those things were always there, but I couldn't reach them before. The noise drowned everything else out. Now, even when it's present, it doesn't erase everything around it. I don't romanticize this balance. Some days it's fragile. Some days it tips. There are moments when the noise swells and I have to adjust again, slow down again, remind myself of what I know. But those moments don't undo everything anymore. They don't convince me that I've lost my footing entirely. Life with the noise isn't peaceful. It's livable. That's the difference. I can coexist with it without disappearing. I can make choices without waiting for perfect clarity. I can participate in my life without needing my mind to cooperate fully first. Anxiety and depression still speak. They just don't speak for everything. They're part of my experience, not the definition of it. And learning to live with that distinction allows life to stretch out again, to have dimension, to feel like something I'm inside of rather than something I'm trapped by. Life didn't get quiet. It got wider. And in that widened space, I can move, breathe, notice, and live — not free from the noise, but no longer confined by it.

Meaning didn't come back in grand ways. It didn't arrive as purpose or clarity or a sudden understanding of why I went through any of this. It showed up quietly, in places I used to overlook, in moments I never would have thought to call meaningful before. Ordinary moments started to matter again. Not because they were special, but because I was present enough to notice them. A routine day at work. A familiar drive. A conversation that didn't require effort to get through. These moments didn't feel joyful or profound. They felt human. And after so long spent just trying to endure, that felt significant. I stopped looking for meaning in outcomes. I used to think meaning had to be attached to achievement or direction, to some larger narrative about where my life was going. Now it feels closer than that. Meaning lives in participation. In showing up without forcing myself. In letting moments exist without immediately evaluating whether they're worth anything. There are times when I catch myself engaged without realizing it. Focused on a task. Listening without drifting. Existing inside a moment without monitoring my own thoughts.

Those moments don't last forever. They don't need to. Their presence reminds me that life is still happening around me, even when my mind is busy elsewhere. That wasn't always accessible to me. For a long time, everything felt distant, like I was watching my life from the outside. Now, even with anxiety and depression still present, there are moments when I feel rooted again. Not anchored to a purpose, but grounded in the reality of what's in front of me. Meaning doesn't feel heavy anymore. It doesn't feel like something I have to find or earn or justify. It feels like something that emerges naturally when I stop resisting my own life. When I let myself be where I am without demanding that it lead somewhere specific. I don't need every day to matter. I just need some moments to feel real. And those moments show up in small, unremarkable ways. In consistency. In familiarity. In the simple fact of being engaged enough to notice that I'm still here, still participating, still connected in ways that don't require explanation. Living starts to feel less like a task. Less like something I have to push through or manage carefully. More like something I can inhabit again, even if it doesn't always feel easy. Meaning doesn't replace struggle. It exists alongside it, quietly, steadily, without asking to be recognized. That's enough for me now. I don't need my life to feel important. I need it to feel lived. Learning to find meaning in the ordinary not because it's inspiring, but because it's real gives me something solid to stand on in a life that continues, imperfect and ongoing.

Engagement doesn't come naturally to me anymore. It's not instinctive the way it once was. It's a choice I make, often quietly, often without ceremony, sometimes without much enthusiasm at all. I don't wake up feeling pulled toward life. I wake up deciding whether I'm willing to step into it anyway. Most days, I am. That decision isn't rooted in confidence. It isn't based on believing things will go well or that I'll feel good once I start. It's based on knowing what happens when I don't engage. When I withdraw too much. When I let myself hover on the edge of my own life instead of participating in it. I've learned that avoidance feels safer than it actually is. Pulling back seems like protection, but over time it shrinks my world in ways I don't notice right away. Engagement, even when it's uncomfortable, keeps my life open. It keeps me connected. It keeps me from disappearing into the quiet spaces where anxiety and depression do their best work. So I choose to engage. I go to work even when it doesn't feel fulfilling. I show up in relationships even when I don't feel fully present. I participate in my days even when part of me would rather stay disengaged and untouched. That participation isn't perfect. It's uneven. It's sometimes resentful. But it's real.

I don't wait for guarantees anymore. I don't wait until I feel certain that engaging will be worth it. I don't wait until I know how the day will unfold or how I'll feel by the end of it. I've learned that certainty was never promised, even before all of this. I just didn't notice how much I relied on it. Now, I move forward without it. Choosing engagement doesn't mean I ignore my limits. It doesn't mean I push myself into situations that overwhelm me or pretend I'm capable of everything I once was. It means I stay involved at the level I can manage, without turning withdrawal into my default. Some days, engagement looks small. It looks like staying present in a conversation instead of checking out. It looks like completing a task without rushing through it just to be done. It looks like letting myself be part of the world, even quietly, even imperfectly. Other days, it looks like effort. Effort without motivation. Effort without payoff. Effort without reassurance that it's leading anywhere meaningful. Those days are harder, but they matter just as much. They remind me that living isn't always about feeling alive. Sometimes it's about choosing not to opt out. I don't frame this as resilience. I don't tell myself I'm strong for doing this. I see it as commitment. Commitment to my life as it is, not as I wish it would be.

Commitment to staying engaged enough that my world doesn't collapse inward on itself. There's no promise attached to this choice. Engagement doesn't guarantee joy. It doesn't guarantee progress. It doesn't protect me from hard days. What it does is keep me connected to my own life, even when it's uncomfortable, even when it's quiet, even when it feels unfinished. And that connection, fragile as it sometimes feels, is what allows living to continue — not dramatically, not heroically, but steadily, one decision at a time.

I don't define my life by how little anxiety or depression I have anymore. That measure never worked, and it kept me waiting for a version of myself that may never arrive. If I used silence as the requirement for living, I would still be standing still, watching life pass without me. So, I've changed the definition. Living now means being here even when my mind is loud. It means continuing even when things feel heavy. It means allowing life to move forward without demanding that it feel good first. I don't need my internal world to be calm in order for my external life to continue. This is where I stand now. Not healed in the way people expect. Not finished. Not free from struggle. But alive, present, and participating in my own life.

Anxiety and depression didn't win because they're still here. They didn't win because I learned how to live alongside them instead of letting them decide everything. They didn't win because life didn't stop. I kept going. I adapted. I stayed. That matters. Life going on doesn't feel dramatic. It feels steady. It feels like waking up and showing up, even on days when I'd rather not. It feels like learning that this is simply how I live now — not as a defeat, but as a reality I can work within. I don't fight my life anymore. I don't treat every hard day as a setback or every symptom as a sign that I'm failing. I understand now that this is ongoing, that living isn't something you arrive at fully formed. It's something you practice. Something you return to. Something you choose again and again, even when it looks different than you expected.

This book doesn't end with hope in the way people usually want it to. It ends with honesty. I'm still here. I still have a life. And learning all of this didn't teach me how to escape anxiety and depression — it taught me how to live without letting them take everything. Life must go on. Not because it's easy. Not because it's fair. But because it's mine. And that's enough reason to stay engaged, to keep showing up, to keep living — not perfectly, not fearlessly, but fully enough to call it a life. This isn't a conclusion. It's a continuation. And for the first time in a long time, that feels like something I can live with. This is all how I ended up "Learning How To Breathe Again"!!

The End

RESOURCES

Help is Available

If you are struggling, feeling overwhelmed, or thinking about hurting yourself, you don't have to carry it alone. Help is available, even if reaching out feels hard.

<u>988 Suicide & Crisis Lifeline</u>
Call or text 988 anytime
Available 24/7 • Free • Confidential

<u>Crisis Text Line</u>
Text HOME to 741741
Connect with a trained crisis counselor anytime

Additional Support
National Alliance on Mental Illness (NAMI)
www.nami.org

"A Note from the Author"

Reaching out doesn't mean you're weak.
It doesn't mean you've failed.

It means you're human.
You deserve support whether you're in crisis or just quietly struggling. If one option doesn't feel right, try another. Help doesn't have to look one specific way.

You are not alone.

Words From The Author

I wrote this from lived experience, not from theory or answers. My work comes from learning how to live with anxiety and depression after realizing they weren't temporary visitors, but something I would have to understand and adapt to over time.

Learning how to Breathe Again is my first book. It wasn't written to explain mental health or offer solutions. It was written to tell the truth about what it feels like to lose yourself, to survive quietly, and to slowly learn how to live again without waiting to feel "fixed."

I live a private life, continuing to work, show up, and move forward one day at a time, alongside anxiety and depression rather than in opposition to them. Writing is how I process, how I make sense of what I've lived, and how I create connection for others who may not yet have the words for their own experience.

If this book helps even one person feel less alone, then it has done what I hoped it would.

Made in the USA
Coppell, TX
08 June 2026

78923583R00125